THROUGH A GLASS DARKLY

WILLIAM BOELHOWER

Through a glass darkly:

ethnic semiosis in american literature

New York   Oxford

OXFORD UNIVERSITY PRESS

1987

Oxford University Press

Oxford   New York   Toronto
Delhi   Bombay   Calcutta   Madras   Karachi
Petaling Jaya   Singapore   Hong Kong   Tokyo
Nairobi   Dar es Salaam   Cape Town
Melbourne   Auckland

and associated companies in
Beirut   Berlin   Ibadan   Nicosia

First edition published in 1984 by Edizioni Helvetia, Venice, Italy.

This edition published in 1987 by Oxford University Press, Inc.,
200 Madison Avenue, New York, New York 10016

Library of Congress Cataloging-in-Publication Data
Boelhower, William Q.
Through a glass darkly.

Bibliography: p.
1. American literature—Minority authors—History
and criticism.   2. American literature—Foreign
authors—History and criticism.   3. Ethnic groups in
literature.   4. Ethnicity in literature.   5. Semiotics
and literature.   6. Ethnology—United States.   I. Title.
PS153.M56B64   1987   810'.9'8   86–23536
ISBN 0–19–504194–1
ISBN 0–19–504195–X (pbk.)

2 4 6 8 10 9 7 5 3 1

Printed in the United States of America

FOREWORD

The Ling Liang Church (or Grace Church) at 173–175 East Broadway in New York City has a large sign that reads: "Come unto me, all ye that labour and are heavy laden, and I will give you rest." The text comes from Matthew 11:28. It is the same passage that inspired Emma Lazarus' Statue of Liberty poem, "The New Colossus" (1883), and that gave hope to the hero of Israel Zangwill's drama *The Melting-Pot* (1908), the play which made its title a by-word in America. As if to intensify the polyethnic connectedness, the very building of the Chinese-American Church originally housed the largest Yiddish daily in New York, Abraham Cahan's famous *Forward*. How are we to read such signs, to understand this country of palimpsests?

This book redirects our question in such a way that sign systems and palimpsests appear in a new relationship to the spectator who gazes at them as if through a glass darkly. William Boelhower captivates the reader with a prolonged exegesis of Henry James's *American Scene* (1907), focusing on its famous (though often misunderstood) meditation upon the great "ethnic question" and the cauldron of the "American" character. At the center of James's play of the eyes, there is no American entity or ethnic content, but a *dynamic* relation; no static siding with the major paradigms of assimilation or pluralism, but a balancing in the volatile realm of questions. James's understanding of the ethnic stare, in which the subject is as important as the object, becomes the central metaphor through which

Boelhower asks us to rethink the related problems of ethnicity and of the nature of American culture, drawing on a great variety of texts from Crèvecoeur's *Letters from an American Farmer* (1782), Chief Joseph's (Heinmot Tooyalaket's) 1887 speech, and O. E. Rølvaag's *Giants in the Earth* (1927), to N. Scott Momaday's *The Names* (1976), Maxine Hong Kingston's *The Woman Warrior* (1977), and Toni Morrison's *Song of Solomon* (1978).

Like Fredrik Barth, Gudrun Birnbaum, Abner Cohen, Anthony Smith, and other critics of the ethnic revival, he questions studying ethnicity as if it were an essence or a pure substance. Nothing is "pure" in America—or in the modern world, for that matter. Yet energetic and delightful though the ethnic mix is in American music and popular culture, in books and in movies, in videos, maps, murals, and buildings, the dominant perception in the United States is still shaped by the romantic ideal of ethnic purity or of pseudo-national cultures in a supposedly anomalous polyethnic nation-state. As Benedict Anderson recently reminded us, 1987 is the bicentennial of the nation-state, but ethnically homogeneous countries have largely remained a fiction, while polyethnicity has remained the unrecognized rule and diversity has proliferated. Yet even advocates of seemingly heretical multi-ethnic approaches are too easily inclined to take nationalism's existence for granted and view it as "natural," not as a historical construct.

This is where a concern for ethnicity as a sign system offers a much-needed dialectical corrective. Applying semiotics, with a range of references from Umberto Eco to Michel Serres, to the study of American ethnicity, Boelhower breaks new ground and provides a new model for an understanding of American texts. Stressing semiosis as the production of ethnic signs, he argues that "advocates of the multi-ethnic paradigm now often repeat the essentialist errors of their monocultural predecessors in attempting to trace out a blueprint of clear and distinct and ultimately reified ethnic categories." Instead, he raises the question: "Who can predict when the ethnic difference will surface and

2

why?" He upsets the currently popular ideas about the American literary canon, held both by traditionalists and by ethnic challengers; call attention to the culture of the map and the creation of the grid as the basis of urban and rural America; punctures myths of purity; emphasizes the importance of Puritan origins and biblical texts for American ethnogenesis; and asks literary theorists to question the relational nature of their own textual selections and interpretive strategies. Among Boelhower's many interesting conclusions is the following insight:

> While there is a reasonably definable encyclopedic core to every ethnic culture, it is theoretically impossible to define its intensional limits. As long as there is an ethnic subject, any object can function as ethnic even in a non-ethnic context.

For Boelhower, "there is no parthenogenesis of ethnic codes. One ethnic novel or a particular encyclopedia does not account for the production of another." Therefore, "there is no unilateral aesthetic starting point for the multi-ethnic critic." This book persuades its readers that encyclopedic cataloguing of the supposed "contents" of ethnic groups is futile, since what matters more is the context of the readers' own "gaze." It is what Georges Devereux has termed the "dissociative" identification ("A ≠ non-A") that makes ethnicity emerge, that produces "ethnogenesis"—even though the results of such dissociative gazes may drape themselves in cultural encyclopedias to make the distinction appear more natural. Put to a practical service, Boelhower's model encourages American writers, teachers, students, and general readers to abandon the idea that "mainstream" and "ethnic" texts can be meaningfully separated: the ethnic sign is everywhere, and ethnic writing *is* American writing. This is nowhere more apparent than in the pervasiveness of biblical rhetoric which Boelhower identifies and to which he alludes throughout, from the American eagle in Exodus 19:4 to Paul's letter to the Corinthians that appears in the title. Per-

3

haps, Puritans and ethnics form only another facile opposition, since the early New England settlers succeeded "in making everything like themselves" (William Carlos Williams).

If we followed *Through a Glass Darkly* and approached American literature, "ethnic" or "mainstream," with an awareness of the dynamic nature of ethnogenesis, we might arrive at an understanding of writing as more than a reflection of ethnically diverse "experiences." Instead, literature could become recognizable as a productive force that may Americanize *and* ethnicize readers, listeners, or other cultural participants. It is precisely this aspect that has often been described by American writers who, from the Jewish American assimilationist Mary Antin to the black nationalist Malcolm X, have emphasized the importance of reading in their ethnic conversion experiences.

It is Boelhower's merit to have rediscovered the dynamic and productive side of American literature and to have challenged the untenable—yet widely adhered to—distinctions between mainstream and ethnic writing. With its breadth of scope and implications, *Through a Glass Darkly* is a challenge and an inspiration to readers interested in American literature, culture, and history, in nationalism, ethnicity, and immigration, or in the meaning of maps for the invention of "America." William Boelhower's book also addresses contemporary literary theorists whose recent structural concerns with otherness, difference, naming, and signs could be redirected and historicized with the help of his examples, his readings, and his models. No matter where we stand, this is a book that forces us to question our own ways of looking—if ever we do want to see face to face.

Werner Sollors
Harvard University

ACKNOWLEDGMENTS

It is a pleasure to thank all of my friends and colleagues of the American Institute of the University of Venice for their kind interest in my work; for offering criticism, bibliographical clues, and those rare intuitions that seem to spring gratuitously from animated conversation. My deepest obligation is to Sergio Perosa. Not only has he allowed me to teach a number of courses on various aspects of American ethnicity over the past three years, but his understanding, counsel, and encouragement have been invaluable to me. I also wish to thank Rosella Mamoli Zorzi without whose generous assistance (both critical and practical) my research would never have seen the printed page. Since we spent many rewarding Friday mornings together conducting a course on the description of nature in America literature, I also wish to thank Silvana Cattaneo who will surely recognize some of the ideas advanced here. Finally, I wish to thank my students, many of them now graduated, whose enthusiasm, scepticism, and desire to begin from the beginning gave my teaching and research an immediate context and purpose. This book is dedicated to Franca.

W. B.

TABLE OF CONTENTS

INTRODUCTION

When I taught my first course on ethnic literature in the United States, my students and I continued to run into methodological problems that pointed peremptorily to broader cultural concerns. It was clearly impossible to explain how ethnic literature functions by remaining at the literary level alone. The course, therefore, was mostly about preliminary cultural contexts within which ethnic literature could be identified as such. Indeed, the subject inevitably became ethnic discourse and ethnic semiotics, since the ethnic *verbum* proved to be too diffuse and scattered to be limited to this or that novel or to a clearly defined literary canon. We were also more interested in enlarging the corpus of ethnic texts than in reducing it.

Ultimately, it was necessary to construct an approach that cut across several disciplines, such as cultural geography, anthropology, semiotics, cartography, and cultural history. The course, one can imagine, became a methodological adventure, but above all an attempt to ask the right questions. At the outset there was unanimous agreement that ethnic literature should not be ghettoized by separating it either from so-called American mainstream literature or from national cultural issues in general. We started with the presupposition that there could be no such thing as ethnic literature outside of the structuring context (American political and cultural boundaries) in which it is created, which means that being American and being ethnic American are part of a single cultural framework.

Both subjects (and they are not at all easy to distinguish) share the problem of origins---that great existential toothache for which no dentist has yet been found. In his book *O Strange New World,* Howard Mumford Jones puts his finger on the exposed nerve when he writes:

> Who was this new man, this American? We do not yet know. But finding an answer to Crèvecoeur's famous query dominates our cultural history for decades. (1965: 394).

As great a commonplace as it is, Crèvecoeur's question is the embracing context for any discussion of ethnicity, and as Jones implicitly suggests, there is really no answer to it. The reason for this lies in the fragmented perspectivism of American versus ethnic American seeing and in the dualism of the monocultural and multicultural paradigms. This brings us to the origin of the problem of origins: the perennial crisis of dwelling, of *habitare,* in the United States.

In short, the Americanization of the new world revealed what Andrew Jackson Downing called «one of the most striking of our national traits... the SPIRIT OF UNREST» (Bender 1982: 162). The European voyage to the new continent gave way to perpetual American voyaging, to the Ulysses syndrome; the instruments used by the explorers to identify the American land became the instruments of the crisis of American identity. Having raised his question in 1782, Crèvecoeur naturally connected it with the critical problem of nationhood, implying that both political and characterological boundaries had to be invented in the same process. Needless to say, both the issue of national dwelling and that of creating a homogeneous cultural identity opened up a preeminently spatial problematics.

It was the poet Charles Olson who said, «I take SPACE to be the central fact to man born in America...» (1947, Ital. tr., 1972: 35); and, not surprisingly, the making of the American environment, the conquering of its space, had much to do with making the Americans «a people of Ishmaels» and America an «Ahab-world» (42, 132). Perhaps nobody better than Melville's Ahab reformulated Crèvecoeur's question in its darker ethnic terms:

> Where is the foundling's father hidden? Our souls are like those orphans whose unwedded mothers die in bearing them: the secret of our paternity lies in their grave, and we must there to learn it. (1981: 499).

But America was conceived in predominantly spatial terms even earlier than the eighteenth century mostly because Renaissance explorers, thanks to the technical revolution in navigational science, were able to convert an old chronological myth into a geographical reality. Already in the sixteenth century, American space became a kind of cognitive clay for Europeans to mould a *novus ordo seclorum,* as it says on the American dollar bill. Equipped with their rational technics, they could indeed believe once again in the practical quest for utopia, and the culture of the scale map proved that more than mere belief was involved.

The scale map presents itself as the natural text for a study in American ethnogenesis; it is the major Euro-American narrative link, the geopolitical blueprint that made America a project, an idea, an ideal before it was even a fact. If culture is a way of seeing, doing, and structuring things, if every society is a world-building enterprise, then there is no better locus than the mindscape of the map to study the soul and body of American identity, the American as both *homo loquens* and *homo faber* (Rossi-Landi 1968: 150-56). For it is ultimately the technics of the map (that of binding together) that led to

11

American continentalism and a virulent version of geographical determinism.

As Lewis Mumford explains in *Art and Technics,* «[T]echnics is not just a way of running to and fro and seeking out many inventions: it is a means of creating a human personality more capable of meeting the forces of nature on even terms and more capable of directing rationally its own life» (1952: 55). The time of America is quintessentially the time of technics, and the culture of the map ideally expresses the American as both symbol-maker and toolmaker. Only such a scientifically skilled cartographer could establish a politics of western expansion as a general law and write his culture insouciantly across a huge *terra incognita.*

The geographical strategy of the map, read as a system of visual communication, is directly responsible for the American's conception of time and place in their social dimension. Obviously, «visual» space implies not only what one sees but also what one knows and remembers. «Routes and places are transformed into memories, time and place become the history of one's existence,» Rudolf Schwartz says (Norberg-Schulz 1971, Ital. tr., 1982: 53). But the law of conquest written in the map also organizes cultural ambitions and possibilities, making it possible for Robert Frost to write his famous lines:

> The land was ours before we were the land's
> . . . .
> Possessing what we still were unpossessed by,
> Possessed by what we now no more possessed.
> («The .Gift Outright»).

Here, then, is the great American dilemma as well as the source of the ethnic *scrupulus.* Presuming that he was projecting his cultural values on an empty space, a *tabula rasa,* the «possessed» Euro-American could not but begin his American experience with a difference to be removed, tamed, and cancelled. The initial confrontation between the Indians and the first Europeans set the pattern and the typology of the basic American cultural dynamics of unity versus diversity. The need to make the land politically and culturally one, therefore, is the larger story, the embracing context, of ethnic discourse. The scandal of the ethnic factor lies in that «something» which Frost speaks of in «The Gift Outright»:

> Something we were withholding made us weak
> Until we found out that it was ourselves
> We were withholding from our land of living....»

If my second chapter is about the logocentric organization of the land according to the canons of American identity, my third chapter explains more fully why this technomic scheme could never really be Frost's «gift outright,» why the drama of mapmaking is coterminous with the problem of foundations. «True culture must grow up with the ground,» Frank Lloyd Wright says in his *Autobiography* (1977: 351), but the decision to descend, to land on the local place, is etymologically an act of *katastrophé,* of falling into origins. Here the American self, stripped of his nomadic velocity and synoptic cartographic vision, must inevitably face his forgotten self---through a glass darkly. In fact, ethnic semiosis is ultimately organized on the basis of a topological system that generates an open series of such binary isotopies as old world/new world, emigrant/immigrant, ethnic/non-ethnic, presence/absence, origins/traces, dwelling/nomadism, house/road, orientation/disorientation. This spatio-temporal perspectivism provides not only a way of seeing but also a way of thinking that has its own type of ethnic *savoir-faire.* Ethnicity, therefore, is the major filter for evaluating and criticizing American cultural flight.

A final note: since ours (my students' and mine) was necessarily a methodological adventure, I wish to acknowledge a deep indebtedness to the specialists of the various disciplines we interrogated, perhaps at times even too hastily. The reader, no doubt, will have to be the judge, but hopefully he/she too will be caught up by the excitement of covering new ground. (All translations into English are mine.)

THROUGH A GLASS DARKLY

CHAPTER ONE

A MODEST ETHNIC PROPOSAL

«For now we see through a glass, darkly; but then face to face: now I know in part; but then shall I know even as also I am known.»
(1 Corinthians 13, 12)

The issue of ethnicity in the United States inevitably surfaces at the national level whenever the ideology of the American Dream or of Americanism *tout court* malfunctions or hyperfunctions or simply comes in for such routine scrutiny as the presidential elections. In between times, almost everywhere in America it remains the great unknown local fact. Given the continuing success of the founding political experiment, during which the Enlightenment words of constitutional guarantee were forever fixed and sealed, the issue itself remains somewhat of a scandal---for mere repetition of the alchemical formula *E PLURIBUS UNUM* would not really convert the base metals of a pluralistic society into a finely beaten national gold. Yet this is the impossible possibility, the asylum foundation, on which Enlightenment and even contemporary America is built. It is necessary to know that by definition the American belongs preeminently to the genus *citoyen* (he is above all a political animal), while ethnicity is his specific difference. Only the genus legitimizes his global circulation within national boundaries. Cultural differences within them remain territorially local. Thus, during a recent television debate involving democratic candidates for the presidency, Jewish-American journalist Marvin Kalb attacked Jesse Jackson with these words: «What we can't understand is if you are a black who happened to be born in America or an American who was born black.» Obviously aware of the ideological teeth treacherously hidden in Kalb's trap, Jackson simply danced through it like an ethnic Pan by repeating the quintessential American paradox: «I'm an American born inside a black.» Black American, Italian American, Jewish American, Spanish American, Chinese American, Vietnamese American, Native American---where should one put the accent? On the adjective or the noun, or are both to be read as nouns? The predictive predicament of American behavioral expression is as complex as it is perennial.

On his visit to Ellis Island in 1904, Henry James, certainly one of the most acute framers of what he called «the great 'ethnic' question,» left the scene with a metaphysical *feritas,* saying that he had «eaten of the tree of knowledge, and the taste will be for ever in his mouth» (1968: 120, 85). What caused «the new chill in his heart» was knowledge that he had «to share the sanctity of his American consciousness, the intimacy of his American patriotism, with the inconceivable alien» (85). It is worth hearing James out in full, for in 1980 alone more than 1.25 million foreigners took up residence in the United States, thus matching the levels reached in the first decade of this century and corroborating the novelist's voiced presentiment of the same period: «The after-sense of that acute experience, however, I myself found, was by no means to be brushed away; I felt it grow and grow, on the contrary, wherever I turned: other impressions might come and go, but this affirmed claim of the alien, however immeasurably alien, to share in one's supreme relation was everywhere the fixed element, the reminder not to be dodged» (85). As any student of the American Revolution knows, one's «supreme relation» is with one's country and beyond it no people with pretensions to nationhood will ever go. If the updated image that the age demanded «of its accelerated grimace» (Pound, «Hugh Selwyn Mauberley») became the melting pot, the basic scandal Kalb would hint at remained, almost *verbatim*, the same. Jame asks, «Which is the American, by these scant measures?---which is *not* the alien, over a large part of the country at least, and where does one put a finger on the dividing line, or, for that matter, 'spot' and identify any particular phase of the conversion, any one of its successive moments» (124)?

Two Paradigms, One Problem

Since Oscar Handlin's book *The Uprooted* (1953), it is common knowledge that immigration, far from being a peripheral matter, is the very history of America. In the words of David Potter, «Unlike most nationality groups in the world today, the people of the United States are not ethnically rooted in the land where they live» (1975: 229). This situation has led to a permanent «identity crisis» which the coiner of that term, Erik Erikson, attributed to «the experience of emigration, immigration, and Americanization» (Gleason 1981: 31). Until the instauration of a new multi-ethnic paradigm in the 1960s (Boelhower 1982: 219-30) — and none the less problematical than the preceding monocultural matrix—a super-identity was projected as the solution to ethnic anarchy. It now seems evident that the two extremities of the yardstick used to determine cultural citizenship, namely assimilation and pluralism, correspond to the unilinearity of the two paradigmatic ideologies, and on this basis it is easy to agree with those who claim that the fault lines of conflict in America are invariably ethnic (Birnbaum 1983: 45; Rothschild 1981, Ital. tr., 8, 41). Yet, the basic question regarding the real nature of ethnicity is equally shared by both paradigms and both intend the ethnic factor as a *distinctio,* as an absolute principle of exclusion and inclusion. In fact, advocates of the multi - ethnic paradigm now often repeat the essentialist errors of their monocultural predecessors in attempting to trace out a blueprint of clear and distinct and ultimately reified ethnic categories. According to the monocultural or assimilationist paradigm, one begins by looking through a glass darkly; but thanks to the melting pot process, everybody in America will eventually see face to face — as Americans. This, after all, is the soteriological backbone of the American Idea. According to the multicultural or pluralist paradigm, only by exalting ethnic face-work will United Statesers be able to strip away the rigid American mask and see face to face.

But what Kalb did not understand and James did is that neither the concept of «American» nor that of «ethnic» is separately definable, for neither is an immediately given or individual entity in itself. On the contrary, what stands out as a suitable definition to the question «what is an American» is not the answer but the question itself. Those who really expect an answer, and they are the majority since both paradigms are desperately trying to see face to face (whether it be with one's political and juridical neighbor or with one's immigrant grandparents), deserve no better answer than the one a person received when he asked Louis Armstrong for a definition of jazz: «Honey, if you don't know what it is I can't tell you.» Americans and ethnics in America are doomed to see through a glass darkly, doomed to the vicious circle of their own question and answer format. In *The American Scene,* however, James offers a simple but revolutionary bypass to the progressive «now... but then» fable of Paul the Apostle's First Letter to the Corinthians by abandoning the sacred rage of theory for simple method, by abandoning problem-solving for a hermeneutical problematics, in short, by accepting as positive the inevitability of the circle. The new scripture, which will serve as a working hypothesis for all I have to say in these pages, goes as follows:

> He had been, on the Jersey shore, walking with a couple of friends through the grounds of a large new rural residence, where groups of diggers and ditchers were working, on those lines of breathless haste which seem always, in the United States, of the essence of any question.... To pause before them, for interest in their labour, was, and would have been everywhere, instinctive; but what came home to me on the spot was that whatever more would have been anywhere else involved had here inevitably to lapse.
>
> What lapsed, on the spot, was the element of communication with the workers, as I may call it for want of a better name; that element which, in a European country would have operated from side to side, as the play of mutual recognition, founded on old familiarities and heredities, and involving, for the moment, some impalpable exchange. The men, in the case I speak of, were Italians, of superlatively southern type, and any impalpable exchange struck me as absent from the air to positive intensity, to mere unthinkability. It was as if contact were out of the question and the sterility of the passage between us recorded, with due dryness, in our staring silence. (1968: 118-9).

It should be remembered that by 1904 James had written such major-phase novels as *The Ambassadors, The Wings of the Dove,* and *The Golden Bowl.* Each work was a wholly new start, a wholly new attempt, to study shifting points of view and complex relations. Indeed, if there is a single impetus behind the Jamesian corpus, then it is surely the very drama, the very process, of seeing.[1] It is this relentless practice of «flying in the face of presumptions» (James 1968b: 90) that he brought to the ethnic question and that causes him to raise his habitually musing brow in the above passage. Here the reader is faced with a *locus classicus* of ethnic interactional behavior, but more importantly with an approach that can be read as a modest proposal for an ethnic semiotics. Almost immediately James discards the realm of the *a priori* by admitting the vanity of generalization (the «whatever more... had here inevitably to lapse»), as if to anticipate Wittgenstein's last proposition in his *Tractatus logico-philosophicus:* about that which one cannot speak, one must keep silent. In this case, silence concerns the very «element of communication» the absence of which can be read in the very tentativeness and jerkiness of James's syntax.

An Ethnic Kinesis

If the play of the eyes is crucial in the above passage, there seem to be no preestablished rules for ordering the actual game of the face-work (Goffman 1967: 5-45). When «on the spot,» the «old familiarities» must be abandoned; there is no aprioristic legitimizing frame for the Jamesian *hic et nunc*. One can even argue that the failure to set up an *adaequatio* between seeing and thing seen marks an implicit abandonment of theory, of the possibility of constructing broad metaphysical-like paradigms. In effect, James calls his own objectivity into question by making contact itself the syntactic subject of the passage. Focalization is «between us» and on «our staring silence.» At second glance, it is not at all clear here who is doing the looking or who is staring down whom. Most likely it is the Italian «ditchers» who save

22

face, for James does suggest earlier that «the alien was... truly in possession» (117). At any rate, the question is now irrelevant because what the passage underlines above all else is the fact that this ethnic *topos* is a conjunctural context; which means that both parties are decentered onlookers, both on the margins. At the center is not an entity or a content or a definable subject, but a dynamic relation, a qualifying energy, in short an ethnic *kinesis* (Sini 1982). Presumably, in the very transaction of gazing there are also two different codifications of the same reality (understood here as the product of an organizing activity). Otherwise there would be no crisis of interpretation or no need to learn how to analyze the American scene from more than one perspective.

As a matter of fact, from the unilateral and decontextualized vantage point of the monocultural paradigm, the American's gaze is obvious, natural, and universal. If the supporters of the multi-ethnic paradigm tend to fictionalize such a stance (since the proliferation and defense of many points of view are essentially deconstructive), they often do so at the expense of cancelling or separating out the dominant paradigm with equally univocal passion. In this way they run the risk of setting up a rival myth by assuming the formal paradigm attributes of their melting-pot predecessors.

James, on the other hand, weaves between both paradigms by dislocating the fixed point of view, by making the relation rather than the immobile subject central. In this way what both paradigms exclude (i.e., the interpretative dynamics of the other), James reinstates, thereby opening up a fluid process of ethnic semiosis. Simply put, there is no American scene outside an interpretation of it, and in the light of an ethnic semiotics, I might add, a costructuring of interpretations. That James actually does suggest such a working hypothesis is confirmed by the strategy of questions he then maneuvers onto the page. Taking up both paradigm programs, he converts them into merely provisional points of view by formulating them as questions without answers. There is nothing conclusive in James's handling of them or no attempt to formulate a definitive strategy out of them, even though he shows awareness of the already codified status of the categories he must inevitably use. Both paradigm interpretations are for him mere shifting points of view, since both necessarily imply a relativizing «for whom.»

It is also intuitively natural for James to take up the assimilationist perspective first, it being the dominant and the more institutionalized order of discourse. Before following him, though, we might note that James first attends to the action, the energy, of the ethnic gaze and only then tries to come to an intellectual understanding of the great ethnic issue. For the method I wish to outline here, this means that the context is all; that no theoretical ordering can ever fly free of the tenuous ground of its own making. Any passage from *descriptio* to *prescriptio* can only have the pragmatic status of an interpretation, which in turn is intrinsically tied down to the moment of ethnic contact.

The Sense of the Cauldron

Bound to this drama of seeing and this hermeneutical circle, James submits himself to the first of what will finally prove to be an open series of musings and questions: «The sense of the elements in the cauldron---the cauldron of the 'American' character---becomes thus about as vivid a thing as you can at all quietly manage, and the question [the great «ethnic question»] settles into a form which makes the intelligible answer further and further recede» (1968: 120-1). Thus does James engage the central category of the monocultural (Americanizing) paradigm, which by 1904 had become a categorical imperative. But he refuses to offer the reader the comfort of a simple repetition or restatement of its essential solution. Instead, he chooses to upset the paradigm's lexicon by using the pincers of quotation marks around the key words («American» and «ethnic») and in this way both defamiliarizes them and suggests that their conventional status is historical rather than ahistorical. His troping strategy then focuses attention on his own «sense of dispossession» (86), but by setting up an I-you pronominal contract with his reader he makes his ensuing identity crisis a contagious public disease.

To make sure that his reader is infected, he asks the inevitable question---«Who am I?»---in its broadest social terms. Indeed, by rephrasing his personally felt alienation in the words of the perennial, but for him ineffable, question of American identity, he implicitly undermines the very foundations of the *E PLURIBUS UNUM* seal. This is the way he draws open the curtains on the ethnic semiotic abyss: «What meaning, in the presence of such impressions, can continue to attach to such a term as the 'American' character?---what type, as the result of such a prodigious amalgam, such a hotchpotch of racial ingredients, is to be conceived as shaping itself» (121)? Were he now to provide the rehearsed answer of the assimilationist ideology, he would close the curtains on the abyss and reconfirm the ruling paradigm of the day. By not doing so, he makes the question itself a scandal, one whose answer is unspeakable. Since it is the costructuring context of the alien that binds him to the question, it must be entertained within that very context or else risk being falsified. As a consequence, the basic difference of the ethnic gaze will have been falsely sublated or simply ignored. If James chooses to live the question, to let the question wander dialogically within its relational frame, it is because the answer can only be echoed back as the ethnic question. The very question that wants an answer (the melting pot) is an intrinsic part of the difference that originated the question in the first place. But let us see how James himself sets up this endless semiosis:

> It is more than a comfort to him, truly, in all the conditions, this accepted vision of the too-defiant scale of numerosity and quantity---the effect of which is so to multiply the possibilities, so to open, by the million, contingent doors, and windows: he rests in it at last as an absolute luxury.... He doesn't know, he can't say, before the facts, and he doesn't even want to know or to say; the facts themselves loom, before the understanding, in too large a mass for a mere mouthful: it is as if the syllables were too numerous to make a legible word. The illegible word, accordingly, the great inscrutable answer to questions, hangs in the vast American sky, to his imagination, as something fantastic and abracadabrant, belonging to no known language.... (121-22).

The New Look, the Lost Word

In this way James anticipates yet another of Wittgenstein's propositions from the *Tractatus*, 5.6: The limits of one's language signify the limits of one's world. There is no American *verbum* that can predict and control the play of interpretations springing from the silent dynamics of the ethnic gaze. The fact, the energy, of multicultural contact precedes monocultural comprehension, and the language that is already forged must defer to ethnic kinesis. But this renunciation of theory for a weak strategy of «contingent doors and windows» (see also James's notion of the house of fiction) is positive cause for further ethnic contact, which is «an absolute luxury» — here to be taken in its etymological sense of excess, extravagance, and superabundance. In place of the rage for a reductive clarity, therefore, he opts for the multiplication of possibilities. Seeing face to face, after all, would mean the end of interpretation and the beginning of the reign of definition. Indeed, if on the one hand James's «inscrutable answer» belongs to «no known language,» on the other, the energy of ethnic/American contact seems to generate the language of identity in the form of an endless production of questions. In the United States, need one be reminded, the great question is ethnic. That is, the semantics of American identity must be built out of the syntax of ethnic materials. The costructuring relationship is all embracing: so we are now back to an American born inside the body of a black, the word incarnate, the political idea given a local habitation and a name.

But in dislocating his point of view to the Italian «ditchers» and to «the rich Rutgers Street perspective» (133), James, as his reader might now expect, is in no hurry to exalt what in the late 1960s would become the multiethnic paradigm. In short, one will find in James's shift no recentering strategy. On the contrary, he reinforces the mobile perspective by keeping on the move and manages next to address the problem of «the unconverted residuum» (124), «the launched condition» (125) of the alien, in an electric car. In this kinetic context he notes, «The carful, again and again, is a foreign carful; a row of faces, up and down, testifying, without exception, to alienism unmistakable, alienism undisguised and unashamed» (125).

This observation is not, as it may seem, a nativist restatement of the Bostonian point of view. As a matter of fact, James is shocked by their *new* look, by the consecrating varnish from the «huge white-washing brush,» of Americanism and is ultimately led to ask, «If there are several lights in which the great assimilative organism itself may be looked at, does it not still perhaps loom

27

largest as an agent for revealing to the citizen-to-be the error in question» (127)? James is speaking on behalf of cultural diversity and within the realm of the plural where the «residuum» is conjugated as it once was by Ahab's cabin boy, Pip: I see, you see, he sees. Of course, the real issue is more serious: «It has taken long ages of history, in the other world, to produce them, and you ask yourself, with independent curiosity, if they may really be thus extinguished in an hour,» James notes, adding, «And if they are not extinguished, into what pathless tracts of the native atmosphere do they virtually, do they provisionally, and so all undiscoverably, melt? Do they burrow underground, to await their day again?— or in what strange secret places are they held in deposit and in trust» (129)?

What is remarkable here and in the earlier passage is the fact that James accomplishes his balancing act of steering between the two major paradigms of assimilation and pluralism by means of the simple strategy of converting the objectivizing confidence of the declarative mode into the subjectivizing hermeneutics of interrogation. His working method seems quite apparent: first statement is bracketed and undercut by the conditional «if» and then its finite sense of closure is burst open by a presumably inexhaustible volley of questions. But the key to this method, its revolutionary aspect, does not lie in a simple act of interrogation or in nibbling away at a central ideological kernel from a mobile position on the margins; rather it lies in deferring the calm language of statement (with its metaphysical and reifying tendencies) to the dynamic realm of semiotic instability.

The Great Myth of Nationalism

In 1904, but also in 1782 with Crèvecoeur's *Letters*

from an American Farmer, most statesmen fervidly believed (as they do today) in the great myth of nationalism and in the inevitable fulfillment of its program (Rothschild: 41-49; Smith 1981, Ital. tr., 14-26). According to this myth, the conquest of nationhood was to lead to, if not be based on, an ethnically homogeneous population. It was presumed that ethnicity would be a neutral factor at the macrosocial level. According to the program, laissez-faire capitalism, with its rationalized bureaucratic state and role specialization, with its glorification of constant change and market mobility, was to produce such a level of political and economic freedom that the ethnic factor would be modernized out of existence. It was the universal liberal belief that such primordial ties as religion, language, and race would disappear; and in its more contemporary version, that technology, consumerism, and the mass media would unify, would cancel, all internal differences. Progress would know no barriers. There would be a single, standardized mass society and Walt Whitman's democratic man *en masse* at the helm. All this we now know simply did not come about. Only the imperialism of an incredibly entrenched world view could have taken for granted that the American, the Western man par excellence, would become a merely political and economic subject, that culture would be unilaterally based on these components alone.

It did not take an ethnic revival (largely the invention of the same paradigm logic described above) to mark the systematic dimensions of the lie. As Anthony Smith has noted in his book *The Ethnic Revival,* not only is it impossible to speak coherently of the United States (or, for that matter, the great majority of modern nations) as a single national culture but also the very designation of «nation state» as a concept of cultural purity is erroneous and illegitimate (Ital. tr., 1984: 19, 26). Furthermore, it is historiographically dilettantish to consider the

29

ethnic question a passing or, even worse, a recent phenomenon, since ethnic consciousness itself is the very product, and not a deviation, of economic development and advanced capitalist society. As a rule, modernization tends to increase differences rather than eliminate them, while capitalism by its very nature generates ethnic protest. These observations will receive sharper focus in the next chapter, which will deal with ethnogenesis in colonial America and in particular in the United States of the nineteenth century.

At any rate, because of his inquisitive way of approaching things, James was not deceived by what he called the «scientific force» (1968: 128) of the colossal machinery (120) of the melting pot, for if we pick him up where we last left him, we find him musing, «Isn't it conceivable that, for something like a final efflorescence, the business of slow comminglings and makings-over at last ended, they may rise again to the surface, affirming their vitality and value and playing their part» (129)? The melting pot for James is not unlike Melville's sea — often glassy smooth on top but underneath seething with unclassifiable variety. He writes, «The cauldron, for the great stew, has such circumference and such depth that we can only deal here with ultimate syntheses, ultimate combinations and possibilities» (130). By speaking from within the plural, by deferring theory to the fishy, elusive detail at the bottom of the pot and to the single fleeting glance of an Italian ditcher, James is able to contact the local, where the American residuum betrays an irreducible ethnic energy; where ethnic *kinesis* reveals itself in the very act of its concealment.

The Ineffable Ethnic Difference

The national category of the global cannot control

its own internal colonies. Who can predict when the ethnic difference will surface, and where, and why, and how? Was the gap between James and the Italian workers social? Perhaps he was dressed in a cool linen shirt and carried a walking stick; perhaps from the ditch they noticed only the polish of his shoes or the fine English fabric of his trousers. And they, it is very likely they still wore their old-world peasant garb. Maybe, though, the gap was economic, a difference in wages, food, residence. Or was it political? In 1904 Italians were often stereotyped as anarchists, socialists or radicals. Were they nurturing some hidden revolutionary scheme? No, more likely the ethnic stare was racial or religious or linguistic (James speaking Italian and they Sicilian) or perhaps only a matter of customary reserve.

The point, I think, is clear: there is almost no way to identify any single ethnic factor. Nor did James care to. All of the above factors can be ethnic and ethnic contact can invoke them all. Well-ordered taxonomies, James seems to imply, pertain to a one-sided paradigm strategy that favors definition and theoretical elaboration, as if a set of rigidly constructed categories could, through description, control the energy of the ethnic sign. James, however, offers a corrective working hypothesis that dwells on the *production* of ethnic semiotic activity, on that unchartable non-space where a sign becomes ethnic. Here lies all the difference and it will be the concern of my third chapter to develop his hints into a local model of ethnic semiosis. The need for such a model can be shown easily enough by repeating Thomas Sowell's recent remark, «In short, ethnic identity has been a complex and elusive phenomenon» (1981: 294). Almost everybody who has ever embarked on the taxonomic quest would agree.

Rothschild lists race, consanguinity, religion, language, customs and practices, regionalism, and political experience as ethnic components (92-99), only to conclude that the identity and boundaries of ethnic groups are very flexible and multiple (132). Smith defines an ethnic group in this way: a social group whose members share a sense of common origins, claim a shared and distinct historical past and destiny, possess one or more distinguishing cultural attributes and have a sense of collective unity and solidarity (114). In keeping with Rothschild and Sowell, however, he too admits that an accurate definition of ethnicity escapes him (29).

Perhaps one of the most important examples of the hopelessness of the encyclopedic approach to ethnicity is the *Harvard Encyclopedia of American Ethnic Groups,* where the descriptive urge is quite exhaustive. There sixteen control features are listed for group entries (1981: viii): origins, migration, arrival, settlement, economic life, social structure, social organization, family and kinship, behavior and personal/individual characteristics, culture, religion, education, politics, intergroup relations, group maintenance, individual ethnic commitment. Nonetheless, the editors are also quick to admit that any definition of ethnicity must remain «flexible and pragmatic.» «The fluid and situational nature of ethnicity makes precise estimates of the numbers of 'ethnic' and 'nonethnic' Americans impossible,» they confess (vii).

Indeed, a single ethnic contact, like James's, or even a single ethnic sign seems to be able to bring the whole descriptive house down. In short, no encyclopedia can pretend to control ethnic sign production. Between inventory and event one finds the same chasm that separated James's working hypothesis from the false presumptions of the melting pot paradigm. In cauldron terms, the difference is between the smooth surface and the boiling stew beneath.

The Realm of Contact, the Local Place

But as a rival paradigm the multi-ethnic ideology is on no more solid grounds when it tries to develop a theory of ethnicity in substantive rather than relational terms. Berndt Ostendorf is quite right in arguing that ethnicity is not «an absolute cultural or social essence (whether genetic, psychological, cultural or social is here beside the point)» (1983: 152). In effect, it is misguided even to speak of a multi-ethnic paradigm if by that one means to claim for it a status and tactics similar to the so-called monocultural paradigm. Of course, with the help of James, I hope I have made it clear that the identity crisis of Americans can only be handled as ethnic discourse, since everybody in America is willy-nilly an ethnic subject. The question «What is an American?» is also an ethnic question for obvious genealogical reasons. I do not mean to say that both paradigms have not served in crucial ideological battles. The point is another. Neither model of interpretation can claim for itself an univocally self-referential foundation. Context and not content must ultimately serve as the epistemological touchstone. Calling on Gregory Bateson, it might even be better to speak of an inclusive «transcontextuality» or contextual structure whereby to act as one of two terms (assimilation and Americanization versus pluralism and ethnification) of a structure of interaction means immediately to summon the other term (1972, Ital. tr., 1976: 295, 298-9).

While attempts to purify research activity by ordering one's investigations in a single direction do ban ambiguity and methodological anarchy from paradigm analyses, in the same stroke they also detach ethnic cultures and discourse from the central issues of the dominant culture. In contact situations, on the contrary, the two domains are indissolubly interwoven, since both are condemned to share the same semiotic space. The only way for the ethic individual to get «outside» of American culture is by burrowing ever more deeply «inside» it, which is basically a movement from the global to the local. Inevitably, therefore, both insiders and outsiders must also confront the same spatio-temporal context; that is, both must confront the common problematic of *habitare,* which I will treat in subsequent chapters. There will, however, only be a valid multi-ethnic paradigm when Americans really decide to discover the authenticity of place within their national space, when Americans really decide to face the problem of *habitare*---which is one with the concept of identity crisis---within their political boundaries. But here we have come back to the genealogical dilemma that underlies both the monocultural and multi-ethnic paradigms and disseminates cultural instability at their very centers.

Mainstream and Ethnic Literature: Uneasy Bedfellows

Mainstream and ethnic literature has also been deeply affected by paradigm decontextualization. Indeed, the long established practice of compartmentalizing American literature into mainstream and ethnic cannot but lead to the belief that they are separable if not separate canons. There was, in fact, a highly entrenched critical tradition based on a consensus matrix that succeeded in establishing a rather untouchable and, I might add, apparently non-ethnic pantheon. In the genre of autobiography, for example, one would most likely find the names of Franklin, Thoreau, and Adams, but not those of Louis Adamic, Constantine Panunzio, and Mary Antin. On the other hand, a contemporary course on ethnic literature might include the last three texts but not the first three. In this light it does appear that many multiethnic advocates have played into the hands of the dominant paradigm's strategy of reductionism. They might argue, of course, that by separating ethnic literature from the mainstream canon, it will finally get its due attention. Yes and no. No, because for the dominant critical matrix ethnic literature in such a framework will remain poor, minor, ephemeral, local, aesthetically inferior, and thus easily dismissable. In fact, this ghettoized version of ethnic literature may even lead to this extreme underestimation of its peculiar identity by Berndt Ostendorf: «Its victory as literature spells its defeat as ethnic culture» (150).

The non-dialogical stance, in effect, is too neat and theoretically assailable. Sooner or later multi-ethnic critics, like their mainstream counterparts, will have to play the rather academic game of literary purity: this is ethnic, this is not. And it can only end up in a bloody tactics of massacre in which a kind of mystic Solomon's sword is used to cast judgment over texts by amputating not only one text from another but one part of a text from another. According to this logic, it is presumed that the sole area where true ethnic signs are produced and circulate is in ethnic literature. But if one sets up such an absolute category, one is then forced to follow the one-way path of the encyclopedia and establish a set of contents as the dominant aesthetic norm. As the Jamesian example has shown, though, there is no parthenogenesis of ethnic codes. One ethnic novel or a particular ethnic encyclopedia does not account for the production of another. In truth, there is no unilateral aesthetic starting point for the multi-ethnic critic; he must learn to be contented with James's tentative *va-et-vient* between the two epistemes.

Moreover, this situation is far from being desperate. Why not, for example, consider the ethnic novel (and I am too sceptical to believe that such an animal really exists) as a novel with a difference or with a play of differences. In other words, it can be ordered by such various narratological programs as the detective story, the pastoral novel, the utopia, the proletarian novel, and so forth, but what distinguishes it from mainstream samples of these literary typologies is the fact that it circulates ethnic signs with a greater or lesser degree of frequency and intensity. The very «ethnicity» of ethnic and, for that matter, mainstream fiction then becomes pangeneric and transcultural.

By avoiding totalizing concepts like the ethnic novel, by transforming issues of substance into a strategy of pragmatics, one can indeed include in his reading list for a course on ethnic fiction such texts as Mark Twain's *Adventures of Huckleberry Finn,* William Faulkner's *Light in August,* and Willa Cather's *My Antonia* along with Ralph Ellison's *Invisible Man,* Henry Roth's *Call It Sleep,* and Mario Puzo's *The Fortunate Pilgrim.* Not only does such a list show how ubiquitous the ethnic sign is in American literature but also how hopelessly American ethnic fiction is. Through such a confrontation one can also avoid reducing the polysemic richness of texts to a mere genre check-up, a practice which has not served ethnic literary discourse well. As I will show in a later chapter, there is a highly codified immigrant narrative regime (Boelhower 1981: 3-13) that functions as a kind of epicenter for ethnic discourse, but it is exactly through a comparison with this text type that one learns how chamelion-like ethnic literary forms are.

The Single Ethnic Sign

It is by giving full critical attention to the highly local ethnic sign (a name like James Gatz, for instance, or Queequeg's tattoos or an involuntary Talmudic gesture by Abraham Cahan's David Levinsky) that one can hope to verify Werner Sollors's remark, «American literature as a whole can be read as the ancestral footstep or coded hieroglyph of ethnic group life of the past and ethnic tensions in the present» (1981: 649). In terms of my monograph, this means that the ethnic sign and the empirical traces of ethnic discourse are so capillary, so pervasive, so inseparable from the mainstream literary corpus that any effort to relieve American literature of its ethnic corpuscles by means of critical blood-letting could only result in its bleeding to death. If this is true, then heuristic tools must also be found which are capable of radiographing how the ethnic subject imposes or positions itself at all levels of the various cultural systems to which it belongs, either as presence or absence. Naturally, such tools should also allow one to go beyond the vague concept of ethnic fiction or it will remain impossible to understand how the ethnic sign is produced. In the end one must return to the local horizon of James's ethnic stare in order to build the foundations of a model of ethnic semiosis with a range that covers both the minimal aleatory trace and the highly institutionalized genre. Ethnic fluency depends on such a broad potential of semiotic reconnaissance.

Where monocultural and genre interpretations flatten the ethnic sign to summary equivalences, for example by canceling the ethnic reading of Upton Sinclair's *The Jungle* in favor of a merely proletarian version, our local model of semiosis shows how a weak ethnic discourse, even by its progressive evaporation, is actually capable of calling into question the totalizing criterion of a genre program. This same ethnic deconstructive energy is also at work in the so-called pastoral trilogies of William Carlos Williams and Sophus Keith Winther, to cite another example of how an entrenched narrative continuum can be resegmented ethnically or, if you will, against the common American grain. The point is, without such a local ethnic semiotics, ethnically embedded signs would often be dissolved in signifying solutions that are more stringent and systematic than they are. At the same time, it is precisely the aleatory and marginal status of the ethnic sign, its virtual uncontrollability and ubiquity, that makes its presence a constant source of disturbance in so-called dominant cultural texts.

Given its normally subaltern status, the ethnic sign's appearance in various fictional genres is often too fluid and unstable to be easily detected and evaluated. If we go back to James's ethnic gaze, we can understand why no encyclopedic set of cultural contents and descriptions, no extensional operation, could explain how ethnicity actually works as a weak or even strong intensional mechanism. After all, James did not see face to face, but through a glass darkly. The sign gaze did not establish a series of semantic correspondences but offered instead an inferencing context. The gaze, the sign, is above all an interpretative relation, a putting into relation. Only for the above-mentioned paradigm ideologies does meaning precede context. By choosing the context, James put himself in a position to see how ethnic semiosis can disrupt the very authority of paradigm logic. Not having the latter's authority to dictate its own terms, the ethnic context modestly implies a different interpretative posture, an altogether different way of looking at the terms themselves. Moreover, the scandal that James revealed some sixty years ahead of time could only have been made possible within the relational structure of the ethnic sign itself. What the Jamesian gaze really uncovered was not the sociological information produced, but the different structural processes behind its production. His choice of the context over the melting pot paradigm was radically innovative for his day and offered *in nuce* a model for rereading all of American literature with an eye to the single ethnic sign.

A sign is only ethnic if it is produced or interpreted

as such by an intending subject. Beginning with it, one can catch a glimpse of an entire ethnic world, for ethnic semiosis, as Umberto Eco helps to explain, carries with it a set of instructions for an interpretative program (1984: 5, 118-20). In other words the semiotic process involves not so much a particular group of things as it does their being grouped in a certain way. It is, in short, a position of reading. In this light the very notion of an ethnic encyclopedia as a rigid inventory of classified data is recast as a complex chain of ethnic sign relations. But this will be taken up more fully in the third chapter. Here I simply want to note that it is the specific type of cognitive gaze that alone generates a cognitive map equivalent to an ethnic world. Consequently, we must begin and end with its relational energy. The only objection that I have to the construction of ethnic encyclopedias such as the very fine *Harvard* volume is that they are so easily used to reinforce the decontextualized and static practices of the monocultural and multi-ethnic paradigms. Indeed, I am almost tempted to conclude that the ethnic sign and its importance have been neglected largely because of such reified inventories. What we really need in order to strengthen ethnic-reader competence is a working hypothesis like James's; that is, a model of participation which will permit us to see the laws of ethnic semiotic production.

For James, the occasion of ethnic contact began with an initial stare and opened up to a horizonless inferencing field. It was this hermeneutical context with its dialogical foundation that allowed him to identify the fundamental structure of cultural differences making up the very spatio-temporal boundaries of dwelling in the United States. On this foundation I will try to build a specific model of ethnic semiotics capable of identifying ethnic *kinesis.* The task will involve establishing rules for determining the major or minor necessity of ethnic implication — in short, rules of institutionality or a grammar of an ethnic system of signs (Eco 1984: 51, xi). But beyond this model, which basically involves a discourse of origins, is the problem of the origins of ethnic discourse. In Eco's words, «The science of signs is the science of how the subject is historically constructed» (1984: 54). In order to explain the fact that American literature is irremediably ethnic, no matter what form the latter might take (latent or manifest, passive or aggressive, involuntary or voluntary), I must approach it genetically. The next chapter, therefore, will be on ethnogenesis or the making of American identity.

CHAPTER TWO

WHAT IS THE AMERICAN?
A STUDY IN ETHNOGENESIS

The Puritans: «The first to come as a group, of a desire sprung in themselves, they were the first American democracy — and it was they, in the end, who would succeed in making everything like themselves.»
(W.C. Williams, *In the American Grain*)

«Doubtless it will be painful to leave the graves of their [the Indians'] fathers; but what do they more than our ancestors did, or than our children are now doing? To better their condition in an unknown land, our forefathers left all that was dear in earthly objects.»
(from President Andrew Jackson's second Annual Message to Congress)

Already in 1782, one year before the Treaty of Paris officially sealed the independence of the United States of America from Great Britain, people in London could read the now perennial question which J. Hector St. John De Crèvecoeur first asked in the third of his *Letters from an American Farmer,* «What then is the American, this new man» (1957: 39)? But the question itself announced the beginning rather than the end of a catalyzing process that would generate much of what we might label as specifically American discourse.

Instead of providing an answer, Crèvecoeur went on to project one, by promulgating a program and a vision that reeked with the future tense: their «labours and posterity will one day cause great changes in the world;» «Americans are the western pilgrims» who «will finish the great circle» (39). In more concrete terms Crèvecoeur's answer would come gradually with the building of the nation. By making America, Americans would make themselves. The first was clearly the more urgent of the two blueprints to be taken in hand, for the geopolitical consistency of the new *patria* was more of an x factor than was that twenty percent of the population in 1790 (the time of the first census) of non-British origins. Thus, Crèvecoeur's prototypical melting pot was a good guiding image for both cultural and political reasons. If diversity and difference were its raw materials, a new nation and a new national identity were to be the constructive result.

In the face of a loosely connected federation of states, with the vast and practically empty Northwest Territory still to be settled and national boundaries not at all fixed, the choice of the national motto must have seemed almost obvious: *E PLURIBUS UNUM.* The image on the national seal, an American eagle, was equally appropriate, and what former British colonist could have forgotten the Old Testament passage from the book of Exodus (19: 4) where Yahweh reminds his chosen people of the promise he had made to them: «Ye have seen what I did unto the Egyptians, and how I bare you on eagles' wings, and brought you unto myself.» The chronometrics of the motto could only have been futurological and, perhaps for that very reason, was religiously heeded as only an abstract, but divinely inspired, idea can be.

In its globality the project was both geographical and ethnogenetic, since it entailed the conversion of a vast topography, with its infinite variety of local spaces, into a single homogeneous national unit. Political boundaries and the ethnocentric *logos* were to march hand in hand, while the two definitions of American identity and American nationhood would be forged simultaneously in the effort to create a single bounded juridical space. But it is enough to repeat that Thomas Jefferson, an expert both in nation-building and in Indian things, is said to have translated the word «Iroquois» as «we-the-people» (Lincoln 1983: 4) to know that Crèvecoeur's question and the everlasting difficulty of finding an answer to it are very old indeed. When asked by an anthropologist what the Indians called America before the white man came, an Indian told him in all simplicity, «Ours» (Deloria 1975: 169). Francis Jennings helps to explain: «The so-called settlement of America was a resettlement...» (Lincoln 1983: 6).

The material problem between Europeans and Indians first and between Americans and Indians later was land, while the conceptual problem deriving from it was that of *habitare* or of two warring conceptions of what *patria* means. Needless to say, what was at stake here was American identity, for without a sense of *patria,* of a homeland, there could be no dwelling; and without a national dwelling, there could be no national character. It is Gaston Bachelard who said that the self is nothing but a diagram of the various functions of *habitare,* the spatial unfolding of the proposition «I am» (1957, Ital. tr., 1975: 42). And, as Heidegger has pointed out in his now classical essay «Building Dwelling Thinking,» in the phrase *«Ich bin»* the verb *«bin»* springs from the root-word *«bauen,»* which means «to build, to inhabit» (Choay, Ital. tr., 1973: 438ff.). From the very beginning, the problem of the Indian in the eyes of the Europeans was a problem of circulation, a problem of connecting a multiplicity of spaces, apparently unrelated, into a single communicational circuit, a unified cultural discourse.[1] Culture-building is preeminently a combinatory calculus and can be read as the structural form which the connecting dynamics constructs. Out of this spatial discourse the image, the personality, of the weaver will inevitably emerge; it is but a question of carrying out what Bachelard called a «topo-analysis» (27). The point is, the building of the American character can be read best on a map as he builds his topological morphologies and stretches his political ecumene over the anarchic disposition of the realm of the local.

Contact, a Cartographic Game of Presence and Absence

If the Euro-American call to order can be summed up in the word «advance,» the native American reaction can only be «retreat» or, in its later ideological form, «removal.» Vine Deloria tells a popular Indian joke that goes like this: «It is said that when Columbus landed, one Indian turned to another and said, 'Well, there goes the neighborhood'» (154). The Indian was the white man's first radical contact with the Other, and the American self inevitably had to be defined in relation to him. The paradigm logic of Euro-American identity also produced the original interpretation of him who, through that same interpretative process, remained the continent's most blatant other self. By this same logic, the building of the American universe left in its wake an ethnic multiverse. In the final count, therefore, we must return to the map as kinegraph (Poyatos 1983: 286ff) in order to discover that the very making of the American answer through colonial advance could only have been formulated as the raising of the ethnic question. The game was (and is) one of presence and absence: but absence here means the Indians' removal from the communitary structure of the self as American and nothing more. The ethnic factor remains as an absent presence within the assimilationist logic of *reductio ad unum*. What interests me here is the topographical process of this logic, or the map where such geographical behavior is written in geometrical and mathematical code. The necessary condition of any interpretation is that there be an interpreter, and the charting of colonial territory, which concerns the culture of the map, cannot but reveal the nature of the cartographer. Another and more concrete way of putting it is Jack Forbes's:[2]

> The Indians are the mirror of the North American's soul. If we want to understand the American and analyze his character, we must discover what he does when nobody is watching him, when nobody can oppose his will; when he does what he pleases. And with the Indians Americans have always done what they pleased without anybody minding. (Hansen & Ranucci 1977: 8).

Throughout the colonial period and on up to the 1890s, it was the Indian as ethnic who raised the first major challenge to the idea of a homogeneous nation and brought about the first deep laceration in the American quest for identity, a quest that eventually led to a permanent identity crisis, for a very simple reason. Every representation of Crèvecoeur's question carried with it and repeated the original ethnic relation of an absent presence as answer. The process of internalizing the assimilationist paradigm also gave place to the writing of American history as ethnic history and American literature as ethnic literature. Thus, the process of acquiring a distinctly American character meant that the very historicity of the American self had to be defined by the ethnic relation. But only in the text of the map can one so visually see to what extent the politics of the global was hopelessly committed to and at the mercy of the local, the removed, the aleatory, the rooted, the placed. The

Indians, whose very origin myths speak of emerging out of the land (N. Scott Momaday's memoir *The Names* being one of the most recent examples), whose very culture is based on the tombs of their ancestors, dwelt holistically in the realm of the local when European explorers, riding the wave of an increasingly self-conscious nationalism, first confronted the new world with the confidence of the revolutionary culture of the map.

The Culture of the Map

Motivating this culture was a scientific episteme capable of explaining why America was an idea before it was a fact and why the American Dream is to this day an unchanged narrative segment lifted from sixteenth-century cartographic logic. American identity, in fact, is fundamentally based on the Enlightenment *ratio* that there exists a passage from the local to the global (Serres 1980b: 19). In the practical terms of colonization, this should not be taken to mean that there is a local and a global dimension, but that the global level was used to explain and control the realm of the local. If we interpret the word «reverie» in the following passage from Bachelard in mapping terms, then we are already well on the way to understanding the more specific version of ethnogenesis which I hope to explain:

> One could define immensity as a philosophical category of reverie. Certainly, reverie feeds off of various spectacles, but, through a sort of spontaneous inclination, it contemplates greatness. This contemplation of greatness then determines an attitude and a state of mind so special and particular that reverie places the dreamer outside of the world around him and in front of a world that bears the sign of the infinite. (205).

While nationalist aspirations and the scientific episteme that made the age of discovery possible did put
the explorer in a *vis-à-vis* relation with the unknown, the
infinite, his pragmatic impulse led him to reduce it to
the rules and the degrees of the scale map.[3] This triumph
of geometry, this abstract territory of the traced design,
then served to represent the increasing territorial wealth
and power of the mother nation. By the time the United
States elected its first president, the above cartographic
ratio was even more explicit. In the words of Michel
Serres, «That which the seventeenth century had fore-
seen---that we would be masters of it [the world]---, that
which the nineteenth had prescribed---that we would transform it---, these philosophical sayings are by now children's
games that we play quite well» (1980b: 100). What
this *ratio* eventually dispensed with was nothing but the
world itself; the world as topography, as a thing to live
in and contemplate, was, like the Indian, a mere problem
of local traffic---perhaps even an obstacle but surely nothing
more than a means.

The late fifteenth-and early sixteenth-century maps of
the world remain the ideal text type for tracing the West's
radical act of removal, the substitution of a uniform
scientific writing in scale for its aboriginal center, the
earth (Galimberti 1984: 44). When European reverie
became a concrete desire for colonial possessions, then
the only thing separating desire and its object was the
voyage. The hero of the day, the European explorer,
then set the terms for the cartographic pact that the
colonists subsequently made with the new world. The
map allowed them to say, «This is mine; these are the
boundaries» (Wahl 1980: 41ff). The prescriptive program behind the scattered national claims of the various
European countries could be summed up in the confident
words of René Descartes, «Give me extension and movement and I will remake the world for you» (quoted in

Green, Ital. tr., 1971). It is within this broad framework that the subject of American ethnogenesis must finally be placed, for here are couched the origins as well as the objective possibilities of its noetic base.

While the first contacts Europeans had with the American Indian did help to establish the terms by which the colonists patterned their unique cultural identity, these contacts themselves were already predetermined by the new geographical mathesis inscribed on their maps. When the white man met the Indian, there was not so much a communicative exchange between them as there was a juxtaposition of two opposing world views, of two ways of perceiving space, and, consequently, of defining the subject's culture of *habitare*. Indeed, the revolutionary tool which the colonists introduced was the factor that distinguished them from the Indians, the same tool that allowed them to introduce themselves in the first place.

Of course, the Indians did not have maps in the same sense that the Europeans did. Theoretically, with map in hand, the latter did not even *need* to dialogue with the Indians, since as a cognitive system the map already implied a radical break with the natural environment the Indians were so mimetically a part of. Rather than describe a place, the *geographein* of the map set the new-world topography ablaze with a project, cast it into a single mathematical and mercantile scheme. Actually, it should be added that the function of the first maps was not at all to report a place, but to impose an *idea* of place on the new continent. And we need only glance at the flags and the ships and the toponyms scattered across them to understand that this idea was preeminently political and juridical. In other words, the map was above all a national signature of possession and a public declaration of the right to settlement. This is ultimately why the colonist and the explorer did not really see the Indian as much as they saw through him.

Topography According to Verrazzano

Topography *in se* was reduced to a utilitarian concept by the European explorers, as Giovanni da Verrazzano's account of his first journey to the new world bears out: «My intention on this voyage was to reach Cathay and the extreme eastern coast of Asia, but I did not expect to find such an obstacle of new land as I have found...» (Wroth 1970: 142). The obstacle, of course, was America because it blocked passage to the markets of China. When he finally settled down to the first known European exploration of what is now the east coast of the United States, he made such notations as this: «We did not find anything of great value in this land, except for the vast forests and some hills which could contain some metal: for we saw many natives with 'paternostri' beads of copper in their ears» (Wroth: 141). Since the locus of the forest, as I shall show, has such symbolic importance in the cultural discourse of the early English colonists, it might also be worth repeating the significant insight into European character Verrazzano unwittingly provides when he notes a bit earlier, «Then we entered the forests, which could be penetrated even by a large army» (139). If they did not yield such materials as pitch, tar, masts and spars, forests in themselves were useless, unless of course for pushing a military road through them. In fact, nothing much came out of Verrazzano's voyage except a series of very important maps with French place-names on them. No one stayed.

This brings us back to another function of the map, that of nomenclature, and in this sense Verrazzano's voyage, as read on Gerolamo da Verrazzano's world chart of 1529, was a success. By inscribing his map with French toponyms, Gerolamo da Verrazzano introduced and traced an initial European cultural continuum over east-coast North American geography, thus making a crucial historical claim. Identity was (and is) very much a question of boundaries, for there could not be a national people without a common territory and jurisdiction. On the map culture, geography, and their mutual definition go together. We might even say that the map generates culture through the naming process inasmuch as it provides a structural base for institutionalizing an implicit, and characteristically national, internal order. The legal claim authorized by the map also legitimizes a cultural model.

The cartographic self encoded in the choice of place-names is a homogeneous and distinctly national, cultural self. In the early 1600s Captain John Smith substituted the world «Virginia» for the same territory that Verrazzano once named «Larcadia» and the resulting map of 1612 made that territory at least temporarily English (see Schwartz & Ehrenberg 1980: 89-95). But this is a question over which wars were fought and it is hard to say which came first in importance, the battle or the map.[4] Both concern a struggle for place without which no cultural or historical orientation would be possible. John Smith knew as much when he wrote in *The Generall Historie of Virginia, New-England, and the Summer Isles,* «As Geography without History seemeth as carkasse without motion, so History without Geography wandereth as vagrant without a certaine habitation.»

Scale Map, Chorographic Map: A Question of Instruments

We need not wonder, therefore, why the Indians were invisible as serious partners of dialogue for the early colonists. What they lacked was a map to produce a rival cultural discourse. «They [the American Indians] are as ignorant of *Geography* as of other *Sciences,* and yet they draw the most exact Maps imaginable of the

50

Countries they're acquainted with, for there's nothing wanting in them but the Longitude and Latitude of Places:.... These *Chorographical* Maps are drawn upon the Rind of your *Birch* tree; and when the old Men hold a council About War or Hunting they never fail to make use of them,» Baron de Lahontan wrote in his *New Voyages to North-America* (Schwartz & Ehrenberg: 132). Contrary to the explorers's maps, which pretended to be synoptic and offered a complete view of the world---such is the inscribed boast of each new map printed in these years---, the chorographic map is concerned with a small fraction of space and concentrates on the specific and the particular, in short, on details (Jacob 1980: 107). The Indian chorographer, it could be deduced, was not only concerned with the merely local but was condemned to it.

The Euro-American, on the other hand, treated the local globally. This he was miraculously able to do because his map represented a new kind of power and a new vision of space. Armed with mathematics and Euclidean geometry, the colonist ordered concrete reality according to an abstract system, ordered it, that is, into a homothetic model which, once reproduced on a map, could be taken in in a single glance. Only on this basis could the earth appear as an indivisible and undifferentiated whole. Obviously this uniform global space is an artificial construct, but used as a cultural gesture, as a tool of colonization, the multiple local spaces of the Indian became simply insignificant. It is, then, the theoretical surface of the map and the practical consequences of its lines that made the colonist farsighted and the Indian myopic.

Visible on these early maps is not only a cultural paradigm, but also an interpretative gaze that objectifies the eye of the beholder and offers an identikit of his desires and possibilities. In Martin Waldseemüller's world map of 1507, which is now considered to be the first to show the name «America,» one finds together with the already explicit legends an even more explicit metanarrative comment in the insertion of a miniature reproduction of the main map (see Shirley 1983: 28-31). On both sides of the miniature there are the two portraits of Claudius Ptolemy and Amerigo Vespucci which flank the two hemispheres of the globe in such a way as to leave no doubt about their technical skills and scientific authority. The main map, entitled «Universalis Cosmografia,» was made possible by the cartographic instruments the two figures are holding. These are the prosthetic devices that made globetrotters out of the explorers and provided *homo europeus* with a new set of eyes, a new way of seeing.

When the Indian and the white man faced each other for the first time, the significant difference in the way they sized each other up lay precisely here. Stradanus (Theodor Galle) seems to have intuited all this when in the late sixteenth century he depicted Vespucci's discovery of America as a meeting between Vespucci and a buxom Indian maiden. With his ship immediately behind him, the explorer, in full military dress, is shown holding a cross in his right hand and an astrolabe in his left while looking fixedly into the receptive eyes of the naked maiden now in the act of rising from her hammock extended among the trees (Honour 1975: 89).

The astrolabe and a pair of compasses equipped the colonist with his theoretical eyes and made it possible for him to present himself to the Indians as a global, theoretical subject. Inhabiting a logical universe based on the Cartesian *Cogito,* the colonist could distinguish between the material world around him and his thinking self. Indeed, if anything, the realm of American matter was an obstacle to his subjectivity and to the world of clear and distinct ideas. The very experience of the colonist's first good look at the new world implicitly registered a distance, and at the same time marked an epistemological abyss between the Indian and himself. He did not need the red man to see face to face. On the contrary, looking into their dark eyes must have been like looking through a glass darkly. More than a thousand words the mathematical calculations of his map, its criss-crossing directional lines and its degrees of longitude and latitude, reflect the episteme which structured him. It is owing to his map that the colonist was somewhat paradoxically able to explain to the Indians that they were living in America and that they were officially called «Indians.» Before the white man the two words did not exist---suggesting once again that nothing exists *extra interpretationem*. So much for the logic of the map; but the moral is that what is written is written. The map could not lie.

If the map put the colonist in the position of Icarus, namely in that divine realm from which all the earth could be seen at a single glance (Prontera 1983: 62), the Indian remained not only attached to mother earth but was also confident in his own way of seeing it. His was a direct knowledge of the terrain, founded on hunting, fishing, and ancestral lore. Territory for him was based on social consensus, his boundaries were natural. Memory and oral tradition and the graves of his progenitors created his sense of place. Distances he measured with his feet, not by written calculation. But then space for him was a local matter and he was concerned only with that part of it which he occupied by his physical presence. The physical eye was his measure. In brief, he was part of nature, a so-called primitive man; which only means that he was not lost without a compass.

Captain John Smith's Compass

The revolution lay in the map and in the new

mathesis that made the map possible, as is evident in John Smith's account of how the theoretical European eye once saved his life:

> He demanding for their captain, they showed him Opechancanough, King of Pamunkey, to whom he gave a round ivory double compass dial. Much they marveled at the play of the fly and needle, which they could see so plainly and yet not touch it because of the glass that covered them. But when he demonstrated by that globe-like jewel the roundness of the earth and skies, the sphere of the sun, moon and stars, and how the sun did chase the night round about the world continually; the greatness of the land and sea, the diversity of nations, variety of complexions, and how we were to them antipodes, and many other such like matters, they all stood as amazed with admiration.
>
> Notwithstanding, within an hour after they tied him to a tree and as many as could stand about him prepared to shoot him. But the king holding up the compass in his hand they all laid down their bows and arrows and in a triumphant manner led him to Orapaks, where he was after their manner kindly feasted and well used. (1970: 32).

If read with an eye not on the object but on its maker, this beginner's lesson in the geographical wisdom of the compass offers an *autopsia* of the European subject. Smith's mapping of the cosmos reveals Smith the cosmographer, and the picture he drew, far from being a mere theoretical discourse, was also the *mise en scène* of an ideology. Besides unifying all the world in its interpretative grid, the map unified knowledge and action. The patch of red that dominates John White's famous map, «*La Virgenia Pars,*» of 1585 is significantly Sir Walter Raleigh's coat of arms. The map, in other words, was a military apparatus, a means of monitoring possessions, a tool of power, an operational scheme. *Terra incognita,* the unknown, was only an obstacle to inscription. Clarity lay in nomenclature and boundaries, not in the feature-less expanse of the forest.

For example, on the elliptical map of 1544 attributed to Sebastian Cabot, we find immediately behind the chain of place-names along the eastern coast of North America a vast interior tract of land that is empty except for the figures of two Indians, a jaguar, and numerous tufts of grass (Shirley: 90, plate 69). The inland scene of the South American continent, though, is more dynamically filled in, for there the conquistadores are depicted fighting the Indians. On Sebastian Munster's map of 1540 («*Novae Insulae, XVII Nova Tabula*») there are mostly groups of trees, hardly no names, and in the northeastern corner of what is now Brazil a tangle of trees with a savage leering out of them. Above his head is printed the word «*Canibali*» (Schwartz & Ehrenberg: 50, plate 18). Given the performative scripture of the map, there is no doubt that the figure of the Indian and the series of trees were ultimately meant to designate an obstacle.

When the white men first met the Delaware Indians, they gave them axes as gifts, but not knowing what to do with them, the Indians put them on a cord to hang around their necks as ornaments. Seeing this, the white men then intervened to show them what the axes were for and began chopping down the trees (Catani 1983: 147). As far as the colonial settler was concerned, however, both trees and Indians had to go. In the woods, where there were no lines or distinct constructive features, the European saw only a blank. Not only was he not able to see in them, but, once in them, there was nothing for him to see. As for the Indians, Smith was exemplarily explicit in his attitude toward them: «But if you shoot but one arrow to shed one drop of blood of any of my men..., you shall see I will not cease revenge, if once I begin, so long as I can hear where to find one of your nation that will not deny the name Pamunk» (1970: 88).

By this time, of course, the broad structural terms of the ethnic relation were well established: it was the cognitive strategy of the map against brute nature. Because he lived in nature, the Indian too would have to be subdued. The intrinsic desire of the mapper is to produce a perfect transcription of the land. Nomenclature reduced the local to the global, created an abstract territory out of its topographical irrelevancies. If the Indian protested, saying, «I am where my body is,» the colonist answered, «I am where my boundaries are.» The Euro-American paradigm was clear from the start; one sees what one knows and what one knows is written on the scale map in homothetic language. Here lies the revolutionary advance that gave birth to the American allegory and its westerly march was irreversible.

But Sebastian Munster's cannibal was more than an object to be toponymically eliminated by further mapping. Once depicted, he also represents a subversive reader in the very text of the map, a principle of disorder. As Michel Serres rightly points out, «One does not exhaust the real, he covers it. He covers it with letters» (1980b: 97). In the blank spaces of the map, where the map is silent, the ethnic factor lurks, and the culture of the map is ineluctably doomed to imperfection, for no perfect ideological transcription is possible. Already in Chief Powhatan's day a significant prophecy was spoken by the Indian orator Okanindge and duly recorded by Captain Smith:

> We perceive and well know you intend to destroy us that are here to entreat and desire your friendship; and to enjoy our houses and plant our fields, of whose fruit you shall participate. Otherwise you will have the worse by our absence.... (1970: 98).

Removed from the map, the Indian with the passing of time became increasingly invisible. He did not vanish, as we now know; he simply disappeared from one carto-graphic representation. The difference between the glob-al map, with its peremptory internal organization and nomenclature of presence, and the realm of the local was, already in sixteenth-century America, the Indian; but it was the presence of this very difference that made the quest for a more perfect map all the more urgent, until the geographical object became utopia itself---a consum-mate form of three-dimensional writing.

An Allegorical Map, a City on the Hill

With colonial settlement, the prescriptive program of the map became both typologically and topologically embodied in the land. «Men carry the land they have inside them to the country they find; they superimpose this internal landscape on the external landscape and both become one,» Rudolf Schwartz writes (Norberg-Schulz 1977, Ital. tr., 1982: 70). If the territorial no-menclature of the colonists could not but reveal old-world sediment---New England, Maryland, Pennsylvania, Virginia---the internal landscape they brought with them, their model of *habitare,* was the Biblical land of Canaan with a New Jerusalem at its center. The text used by Robert Gray to justify English expansion in Virginia was Joshua XVII: 14-18 (Gliozzi 1977: 144), the last verse of which reads: «But the mountain shall be thine: for it is a wood, and thou shalt cut it down: and the outgoings of it shall be thine: for thou shalt drive out the Canaanites, though they have iron chariots and though they be strong.» The colonial advance, in other words, was allegorical. Typologically, the colonists were the new Israelites; as for topology, Edward Johnson explains, «for your full satisfaction know this is the place where the Lord will create a new heaven and a new earth in, new churches and a new commonwealth together» (Miller 1956: 31). And in the more famous words of John Winthrop, «For we must consider that we shall be as a city upon a hill, the eyes of all people are upon us» (Miller: 83).

In order to realize the Biblical vision of the city, of the colonial *Ich bin,* the English also had to carry out a scientific *experimentum* of measurement and calculation (Marramao 1984: 71-79). As the text from the book of Joshua suggests, there had to be a preliminary clearing of the ground before the constructive project could get under way. It is common knowledge that the allegorical *graphein* of colonial history was a linear scenario of conquest and transformation, a very predictable way of accomplishing things from the point of view of the Indian. As Werner Sollors notes, «The achievement of a Christian and American selfhood was always part of the struggle against a heathenish, ethnic 'otherness'» (1981: 654).

Perhaps one of the best texts for analyzing the spatial terms of the allegory is William Bradford's *Of Plymouth Plantation,* where the thematic *vérité à faire* is fully described. One of the major reasons for the Pilgrim removal to America was «a great hope and inward zeal they had of laying some good foundation... for the propagating and advancing the Gospel of the kingdom of Christ in those remote parts of the world» (Miller: 12). Bradford then defines the topological coordinates of the remote: «The place they had thoughts on was some of those vast and unpeopled countries of America, which are fruitful and fit for habitation, being devoid of all civil inhabitants, where there are only savage and brutish men which range up and down, little otherwise than the wild beasts of the same» (12). The narrative logic here is ordered along Biblical lines. The Pilgrim voyage was a didactic project with a prefabricated script, and even before setting foot in the new world, they already had an ethical vocabulary for classifying what they would see. If the Pilgrims were the protagonists of the drama, the Indians were the enemy; if the former were civil, the latter were savage. For all practical purposes, the white men were going to a place that they considered uninhabited, since the savages, being etymologically «of the woods,» did not qualify as proprietors or inhabitants. Like «wild beasts» they roamed about with no fixed abode, it was believed. Not having fences, they could not have towns and without towns there could be no such thing as «history.» Along with the explorers, in fact, the Pilgrims introduced the world of historical events into the ahistorical world of nature, and these events were ethnically saturated. Theirs was the story of a Biblical progress, a historical progression and a cultural advance. Given the nature of the script, Bradford's description of the actual landing could only have been a *déjà lu:*

> Being thus passed the vast ocean, and a sea of troubles... they had now no friends to welcome them nor inns to entertain or refresh their weatherbeaten bodies; no houses or much less towns to repair to, to seek for succor.... Besides, what could they see but a hideous and desolate wilderness, full of wild beasts and wild men—and what multitudes there might be of them they knew not. Neither could they, as it were, go up to the top of Pisgah to view from this wilderness a more goodly country to feed their hopes; for which way soever they turned their eyes (save upward to the heavens) they could have little solace or content in respect of any outward objects. For summer being done, all things stand upon them with a weatherbeaten face, and the whole country, full of woods and thickets, represented a wild and savage hue. (Miller: 16-7).

The scene is one of complete desolation and tribulation (both their bodies and the landscape are «weatherbeaten»), nor could it have been otherwise, given the descriptive dictionary to which Bradford limited himself beforehand. We learn *via negationis* and in an ever broader proxemic order of relations what is missing from the utopian picture, what will have to be built, and what destroyed. Bradford first presents an inventory of the familiar features that are absent: the smallest being «friends,» the largest being «towns.» The scale within which succour is possible is defined along homotopic cultural lines. The largest spatial unit, the town, is also the largest category of social definition. Its morphological opposite is the wilderness. There is no possible communication between white man and Indian for the same reason there is none between their habitats. Forest and town represent two different types of *habitare* and, as we shall see, two different modes of discourse. In Old English «wilddeoren» means «of or like wild beasts.» For the Pilgrims it had an added moral connotation evident in the word «bewildering.» One is morally bewildered if he strays from the path of righteousness. The forest, which was the Pilgrims's wilderness, was both physically and morally a place to get lost in, a chaos, a domain of confusion, the exact inversion of a «goodly country.»

The Road versus the Woods, the Allegory versus the Symbol

The colonial *logos* extended itself ideally in the town, the human-built environment, and colonial self-identification limited itself to the perimeters of the settlement. It is hardly surprising, therefore, that four-fifths of the accused witches of Salem lived beyond the town's bounds (Stilgoe 1982: 52). The colonial town was the best single form for transmitting the combined *savoir-faire* of the religious, political, economic and cultural realms. Its roads represented order and guaranteed as well as directed all levels of circulation. As a topological system, the town fortified continuity, proximity, orientation and, of course, legitimized social identity. In short, it assured an ethnological dynamics of the same. Lacking all this, Bradford's Pilgrims had «little solace... in respect of any outward things.» What they actually saw and what he described clearly made no sense to them, being face to face as they were with the world beyond the map. There was no order in the woods, its space of circulation was the exact opposite of the road. It could not be controlled, movement in it was random, unchanneled, non-Euclidean. Nothing definitive, no definition, could in any way emerge from it. There, only the local existed, the object at hand, the space around the body. As for vision, it ended practically at the end of one's nose.

It was—this space of the forest, this Indian territory— an absolute threat to the spatial scheme of the allegory, to its three-dimensional realization. In effect, the threat represented by the Indian resided in his topological disorderliness: he was nomadic, a beast, a mere body without a soul. A man without a soul, of course, is a monster and a monster is such because it proliferates signs and refuses to be reduced to a single interpretation (Galimberti 1983: 241-46). In the woods terrible things happened to the early colonists, things unspeakable and unexplainable. But if there was a binary incompatibility between the cultural logic of the forest and that of the road, the Pilgrims were smart enough to combine the two into a project for a good, straight forest road. Perhaps they too had read Verrazzano or, more simply, perhaps the allegory of the road was in their genes. Only a spiritual Pisgah saved the Pilgrims from the tyranny of the formless topographical body surrounding them and only the discourse of allegory saved them from the circularity of the symbol. This Bradford knew when he repeated for the third time the now formulaic words:

> What could now sustain them but the spirit of God
> and His grace? May not and ought not the children
> of these fathers rightly say: «Our fathers were
> Englishmen which came over this great ocean, and
> were ready to perish in this wilderness; but they
> cried unto the Lord, and He heard their voice and
> looked on their adversity (Deut. 26: 5, 7).»
> (Miller: 18).

The utopia had to be built out of nothing; this was and is the sacred rage of the American allegory. For the Puritans it meant extending the roads of the town and imposing the *ratio* of the Biblical allegory. In different but parallel ways these two strategies both involved seeing clearly. Until all roads became national there would be no real American nation, no total circulation. Only a land cleared of its forests and covered with roads is really transparent. The colonial and national scripts were one in translating the problem of seeing clearly in the forest into seeing to the clearing of the forest. Bradford's rhetoric of repetition was his way of «seeing clearly» and what is most striking in Puritan narratives as a whole is just such painstaking concern over equivalences and correspondences as his. Félix Guattari and Gilles Deleuze would define the effect of this practice as a *«surlinearité de l'expression»* (1980: 108); herein lies the violence of Euro-American allegorical discourse. As with the map, here too it is a question of scale, of applying a ruling homothetic norm in order to make discourse flow regularly along a single-track and rather transparent circuit. A discourse able to «make it ethnologically new» did not get lost in the gaps and the lacunae thrown up by the world, rather it passed over them---for the sake of a clear beginning and a definitive closure.

It should now be evident that the Puritan discourse of allegory aimed at destroying the Indian not only as body but also as discourse. Both are symbolic; the Indian's way of living and seeing were part of nature rather than technologically against it. He accepted no boundaries that were not natural. He refused to super-impose any. His was a mobile, shifting semantics, a per-formative discourse that made no sense outside of its own local context (Hymes 1981: 80-6). No umbrella term like progress cast a linear mold over his doing and saying. Historically speaking, he lived inconclusively and was all too patient with the paradox of detail. The local was his pragmatic norm. In the face of a westering nation of path-finders and settlers, he increasingly lived away from the main roads and his dwelling place became more and more unstable as the Euro-Americans tried to control his move-ment. Beginning with the Puritans, in other words, another America already existed, and for them the Indian was the prototype of the ethnic other: his space was hetero-topic, his discourse confusing in the etymological sense of *symballein*. In his *opus magnum, Magnalia Christi Americana,* Cotton Mather pronounced words against the Indians which would eventually become an ethnic truism: *«Difficilius invenire quam interficere»* (it is more difficult to find them than to defeat them) (Gliozzi: 410).

In the meantime European settlement continued; the non-place of the road annihilated more and more space and set up a kind of permanent invasion of Indian territory. Thus, at the very beginning, colonial foundations were built on a local ethnic corpse. «The conquest of the In-dians made the country uniquely American,» Brian Swann points out (1983: xv). If this is true, then the problem of American identity raised by Crèvecoeur is peremptorily archeological. The American tragedy lies here: having solved the riddle of ethnic difference by means of the technical perfection of the global map and all that it implies, the Americans succeeded in burying the very clues that would permit them to solve the riddle of themselves. At the heart of the cultural structure lay the archaic. In the twentieth century, Western thinkers would try to recover it, from Lévi-Strauss to T.S. Eliot: «That corpse you planted last year in your garden, / Has it begun to sprout? Will it bloom this year» (see «The Burial of the Dead» section of *The Wasteland*)? In the 1960s the ethnic corpse became an object of cultural seduction, of ideal improductivity. In a society of irreversible technological advance, ethnicity---the practice of digging up cultural origins---is a way of staying behind, of getting off the road, of rediscovering place. Due to the pan-Indian movement, it was popularly acknowledged that the development of American presence was based on a progressive absence of the Indian, in such a way that presence and absence are now indissolubly one in the definition of American identity.

City Space, National Space

The topological model of the above dialectics does not derive so much from Winthrop's «city upon a hill» as it does from William Penn's plan of Philadelphia, where the importance of reading the ethnic question in terms of cultural geography is made strikingly clear. Given the influence it would have in determining the future physiognomy of national space (and national identity), the plan might truly be called the American «by-word through the world» (Miller: 83). By 1683 the famous orthogonal plan was drawn up: a perfect geometrical model of rectangular squares and intersecting rectilinear streets (Reps 1969, Ital. tr., 1976: 188ff, 346). Reflecting the values of the new mercantile economy, it organized dynamic forces into a tensional field and was a perfect technico-disciplinary expression of the possibilities of infinite growth. The grid could be infinitely extended without affecting the basic structural flow of urban circulation.

In order to overcome the static nature of the traditional city with its focus on the public square and in order to transform dead areas into channels of activity, the plan boldly did away with the spatial concept of the center, the so-called urban heart. What it gained by this was a city that was always on the move, that never slept. Penn's orthogonal mechanism, a planned structure, became the first built expression of the new way of life promised by the increasingly explicit colonial allegory. For the time being, the not so latent ideology of expansion could not have found a more appropriate morphological symbol. As a model of cultural geography, then, it is an ideal semiotic space for analyzing the dynamics of early American identity.

At the end of the eighteenth century, when the colonies became a single political territory and the whole population (those who were white and freeborn) its *citoyens*, then indeed the American legislators found it urgently necessary to formulate a territorial program of Americanization. As Roman law teaches, *ubi pedes ibi patria* (Virilio 1977, Ital. tr., 1981: 24); which suggests a strategy of mobilitation and incorporation. Even the Pilgrims knew that the only way to establish clear and distinct boundaries and administrative limits was by constructing forts and towns. The road to nationalism, therefore, became a strategy of building roads, made possible by mapping the American land as a synoptic system of dynamic trajectories. American common sense would eventually teach that from the right to the road one passed to the right of the state. Only the Indians would fail to understand this logic.

On May 20, 1785, Congress passed the Land Ordinance, which ordered the surveying of the western territories into townships that were six miles square. The first really national, cultural form, in other words, was the federal survey and by means of it Penn's grid became

America's. As John Stilgoe points out in his book *Common Landscape of America,* this Ordinance «determined the spatial organization of two-thirds of the present United States» (99). Only a nation with an allegorical script could have presumed that the urban morphology of Philadelphia would serve equally well for Jefferson's ideal yeoman farmer in the far reaches along the Mississippi River. Paradoxically, America's most representative values have always been associated with the topology of the farmer and not with that of the city-dweller; yet, given the hypercodified national scheme, it can truly be said that these two spaces are of equal topological value. Both are American because they belong to the same system of political and economic measurement.

It is the grid that made the United States into a single coherent space, that established a national system of property exchange, control, and command, that made all men theoretically equal. The survey itself was made practicable by Gunter's chain, whose twenty-two yards became the standard measurement for dividing townships into thirty-six equal sections, each one mile square. According to Stilgoe, «No mathematical ratio is more important in the American Enlightenment landscape» (100). With the grid natural space and topography became officially irrelevant. But given the times, local differences of all kinds had to be suppressed in order to build a national *habitare.* With the addition of the Louisiana Purchase of 1803 the American territory was doubled and the need to expand westward in order to organize and establish public boundaries became an urgent matter of national defense. Indeed, the Jeffersonian and Jacksonian presidencies were largely committed to the priorities set down by Washington in his Farewell Address of September 17, 1796:

> The name of AMERICAN, which belongs to you in
> your national capacity, must always exalt the just pride

of patriotism more than any appellation derived from local discriminations. With shades of difference, you have the same religion, manners, habits and political principles.... Here, every portion of our country finds the most commanding motives for carefully guarding and preserving the union of the whole.... In contemplating the causes which may disturb our union, it occurs as a matter of serious concern, that any grounds should have been furnished for characterizing parties by geographical discriminations---Northern and Southern---Atlantic and Western. (Williams, Vol. 1, 1849: 71-2).

Subsequent American history was a long march through the wilderness in search of a national identity. In practical terms, this meant ordering American geography into a single semiotic system. What such a system might be is implied in Jefferson's Annual Message to Congress of October 17, 1803, in which he made two important announcements. The first concerned the purchase of the Louisana Territory; the second the «transferral» of the huge territory of the Kaskaskia Indians to the United States (Williams, Vol. 1: 163-4). The Indians would henceforth live «in an agricultural way,» Jefferson declares. As to what to do with their land, he suggests that it «may yet be well worthy of being laid open to immediate settlement, as its inhabitants may descend with rapidity in support of the lower country should further circumstances expose that to foreign enterprise» (164). The process of semiotic ordering pertained to the mobile line of the frontier---to become, with Frederick Jackson Turner, a normative locus for explaining American identity. The task of converting the anonymous *res extensa* of the wilderness into an American sign was consigned to the pathfinder whose job was invariably to connect, to build roads, to assure circulation, to create continuity, to «lay open.» As Horace Bushnell wrote in his pamphlet *The Day of Roads,* «The Road is that physical sign, or symbol, by which you will best understand any age or

people.... If they have no roads, they are savages...»
(Stilgoe: 132). The Indian, hopelessly local, hopelessly
allergic to the acentric life of the linear road, had to be
converted to agriculture or removed. It was the building
of the modern nation that raised the problem of assimilation, acculturation, discrimination, and ethnic rights
(Rothschild: 51), and these issues, it is now known,
could not be solved either by technical or rational means.
The national script was monocultural, the national character as linear in conception as the federal grid.

The Pioneer and his Onomatomania

Surrogates of American union, the frontiersman,
soldier, and surveyor were the first to mediate between
topographical matter and cultural form. On the map,
which it was their business to make, their toponymic
traces can be read as a narrative of cultural transmission
and ideological reproduction. There too one can judge
how successful they were in imposing the allegorical
logos of *E PLURIBUS UNUM* on a potentially infinite
series of heterogeneous spaces---there where the anonymous world became the American word. Thus, the military township created in 1784 in the state of New York
not only had such names as Homer, Virgil, Ovid, Milton,
and Dryden, but also such catechetical felicities as Unan-
imity, Frugality, Perseverance, Sobriety, Enterprise, In-
dustry, Economy, and Regularity (Stilgoe: 102). None
of these suggest a local contact; all are prefabricated
representations of a closed cultural continuum.

If we look at the early colonial and national maps,
the repetition of the word «new» reveals even more
sharply the Euro-American's onomatomania. Read as a
history of his *geo-graphein,* such place-names as New
England, New York, New Jersey, and New Hampshire---

to mention a few of the larger spatial denominations—conceal an incredible field of semantic tensions. Are they to be taken as points of conservation or renewal? Do they suggest a retrogression or an advance? But no matter how one chooses to interpret them, the basic paradox of their inscription remains, for the system of cultural relations they express ultimately obeys a one-track English lexicon.

In other words, what most toponymical peripli show is the muting of the local ethnic word, either by elimination, transformation or mere commemoration. The axiological tension of the map's kinegraphic transcription lies here, as is born out by a comparison between John Smith's 1612 map of Virginia and Augustine Herrman's 1673 map of «Virginia and Maryland» (Schwartz & Ehrenberg: 94, 122). On Herrman's map most of the Indian names that Smith charted are canceled altogether or at least given English spellings. The Powhatan River becomes the James, while such Indian territorial names as «Mangoags» and «Kuskarawaoks» are substituted by the English «Lower Norfolk» and «Dorcester C,» respectively. The beautiful vignette of the inside of Wahunsonacock's lodge with the chief in council and the large figure of a Sasquesahanough Indian, both of which appear on Smith's map, are removed on the later representation.

The point is, the further west the white man went, the more nationalist the kinegraph of place-names became. If the naming ritual was supposed to impose the power of a political truth on the land, what it actually demonstrated was the truth of a central political power. The national map was absolute because the land was absolutely subdued by it: the road conquered place; mobility shattered stasis into a myriad fragments; regional detail surrendered to topological abstraction; cultural difference to ideological sameness.

Near the peak of this national advance, around the

1830s, present-day Wisconsin became the spatial focus of this rhetorical dissemination, and the scriptural itinerary of monocultural naming that was enacted can be verified along the frontier line that moved across it. Going from east to west, one now finds such onomastic poetry as Harmony, Concord, Eden, New Hope, Union Center, Advance, Union, Union Grove, Junction City, Forest Junction, Mount Hope, Centerville, Unity, and Rising Sun. Along with these, and reinforcing their semantic pretensions, are the settlement toponyms of immigrants, most of them clearly trying to make it new: New Holstein, New Munster, Genoa City, Rome, New Rome, New Lisbon, New Glarus, Columbus, Scandanavia, Hollandale and Athens. Then there are such traditional colonial, Biblical, and national inventories as Plymouth, Mt. Horeb, St. John's, Lebanon, New Richmond, Oxford, Jefferson, and Monroe. As for traces of the once ubiquitous Indian tribes (the Sauk, Fox, Chippewa, Winnebago, Sioux, Menominee, and Potawatomi), there are countless place-names designating both counties (e.g., Outagamie, Shawano, Menominee, Oneida, Kewaunee) and cities and towns (e.g., Tomahawk, Keshena, Milwaukee, Kaukauna, Waukesha, Kenosha). By 1840, however, almost all Indian tribes were removed to the western bank of the Mississippi River. What Indians remained were either scattered or confined to a series of clearly defined and strategically located reservations whose internal space appears even today as a complete blank on popular road atlases. This is generally true of mapped reservation space in all the states, so that only national forests and Indian territory present and preserve an uncodified look on the map. In comparison to the rest of the national topography, few roads if any cut through either of these domains. In spite of appearances, however, both forest and reservation are controlled artificial spaces and can be considered largely commemorative areas set aside for the touristic viewing of nature and the natural.

Lost Origins and Local Ethnic Kinesics

Given this framework, one would be greatly deceived if he thought that the above cartographic representation had actually succeeded in eliminating the discontinuous, the aleatory, and the catastrophic dimensions from its model of cultural circulation. When read etiologically, the place-names themselves reveal lost origins and removed meanings that recount anything but a closed semiotic system of homothetic correspondences. As soon as the map reader questions the map's writing, the microhistories embedded there break out like a cancer all over the map's surface, calling into question its very authority. To interrogate the map is to unfix it, to read it kinegraphically, in which case its static being becomes dynamic process; its towns and cities, kinemes; its boundaries, behavior.

The above toponyms of Wisconsin, for example, are contaminated with the circumstances of their emission and circulation. More specifically, they are marked with the history of ethnic origins, which were presumably left behind as the culture of the map detached itself from the topographical territory. When one interrogates the map, however, he performs a genealogical act that requires him to go through and beyond its own seeing. Thus, as map readers we are back to James in that like him we must go through our own cultural image reflected in the mirror of the map. The etiological question is a question of origins, for on the other side of the mirror---Indian territory---lie the origin of the question and the removed ethnic answer.

By interrogating the place-name of Dodge County,

one quickly learns that it commemorates the first governor of the Wisconsin Territory, who was appointed to office in 1836 by President Andrew Jackson. Like Jackson, Col. Henry Dodge owed his political success to his prowess as an Indian fighter. Dodge, more than anyone else, was responsible for Chief Black Hawk's defeat, which ended in the deliberate massacre of his tribe in 1832. It was Dodge, too, who negotiated many of the treaties by which the various Indian tribes were dispossessed of their land and who saw to their removal from Wisconsin Territory (Alice Smith, Vol. 1, 1973: 260-67). Thus, at its very source the name «Dodge» summons an ethnic other, and its implicit calculus of unity and inclusion inevitably yields to the specifics of multiplicity and disorder. But the name itself, as Alide Cagidemetrio suggests in her fine study *Verso il West* (1983: 9-16), is both a minimal and maximal unit of American discourse, inasmuch as its local ethnic kinesics seeks to impose the global promise of the national allegory. As such the entire script is virtually repeated in the propositional structure of the single toponym.

That this American script is woven out of ethnic cloth can be seen in President Jackson's Inaugural Address of March 4, 1829:

> Our conduct toward these people [the Indians] is deeply interesting to our national character.... Our ancestors found them the uncontrolled possessors of these vast regions. By persuasion and force they have been made to retire from river to river, and from mountain to mountain, until some of the tribes have become extinct, and others have left but remnants, to preserve for a while their once terrible names. Surrounded by the whites, with their arts of civilization, which, by destroying the resources of the savage, doom him to weakness and decay, the fate of the Mohegan, the Narraganset, and the Deleware, is fast overtaking the Choctaw, the Cherokee, and the Creek. That this fate surely awaits them, if they remain within the

limits of the states, does not admit of doubt. (Williams, Vol. 2: 710).

While the names of Dodge and Jackson (also a county toponym in Wisconsin) did substitute the «terrible names» of Winnebago and Chippewa on the map, they did not, and could not, cancel the contextual ethnic sign at their origins; because the very relational structure of cartographic kinesics elaborates the following oppositions: map versus topography, global versus local, continuity versus discontinuity, unity versus multiplicity, order versus disorder, control versus non-control, possession versus dispossession, conqueror versus conquered, civil versus savage, white versus Indian. All these in turn are subsumed under the costructuring categories of American *citoyen* versus ethnic *homme,* the two components on which depends a definition of dwelling in the United States. In order to follow its assimilationist script, in order to legitimize the ethnogenetic process of national identity, the maker of the map must indeed keep up a necessary cartographic fiction.

On the Road to American Identity

This allegorical «keeping up,» this facing down of the Indian, is the phenomenological form of Crèvecoeur's question «What is the American?». The writing of the national *«Ich bin»* can be read as «I am what I have done,» and in three-dimensional terms this is fundamentally a question of cultural geography, a quest for a *patria.* According to the dynamics of the map, there was only one verb to express the process of building a homeland and it was an imperative: EXPAND! The history of the United States is nothing but a series of variations on this theme, to the point that an originally spatial concept, the West, was transformed into an abstract game of circulation. As nation-building was intensified, so was the American form of dwelling---until it extended over the entire national map, and through technical wizardry the democratic revolution became dromatic (Virilio 1981: 46).

When ex-soldier Grenville Dodge, whom the Indians nicknamed «Long Eye» because of the miraculous powers of his instruments, began surveying along the forty-ninth parallel, he hoped to make the first transcontinental railroad a practical possibility. Along with 5,000 soldiers General William T. Sherman sent Dodge this message:

> I regard this road as the solution of Indian affairs and of the Mormon question, and I will help you all I can. You may rest easy that both Grant and I feel deeply concerned in the safety of your great national enterprise. (Quiett 1965: 40; see also 13-20).

As a concrete symbol the road best expressed the American Way of confronting facts, and what this meant for his dwelling and his character, Whitman explains in his poem «Years of the Modern»:

> I see this day the People beginning their landmarks,
>   (all others give way;)
> . . . .
> Lo, how he [the average man] urges and urges, leaving
>   the masses no rest!
> His daring foot is on land and sea everywhere, he
>   colonizes the Pacific, the archipelagoes,
> With the steamship, the electric telegraph, the news-
>   paper, the wholesale engines of war,
> With these and the world-spreading factories he inter-
>   links all geography, all lands.

The building of American identity and a national culture of *habitare* followed the blueprint of the map's circulation, but in subjecting himself to it, the American *citoyen* exposed himself to his own nothingness. The road is a non-place, it leaves the masses no rest. He who follows the national road cannot dwell because the road annihilates place. The global strategy of the map is a strategy of deterritorialization, an aesthetic of corporeal disappearance, for one cannot be ubiquitous and still keep body and soul together. For this reason, American identity is an abstract idea; indeed, such a «nation of strangers» is a society that has lost its sense of place. Without the latter there can be no memory and no identity as these too are tied to place. Nor does *habitare* mean mere circulation, since the road only makes sense if one remembers where he started from and where he is going. In the classical journey both are places (Turri 1979: 51, 55).

In the face of such a dilemma, American identity is condemned to endless questioning, to an endless hermeneutical process, as the Whitman of «Years of the Modern» again reveals. «Years prophetical! the space ahead as I walk, as I vainly try to pierce it, is full of phantoms,» he writes. But his phantoms are not future projects as much as they are the ghosts of the past. The structural weakness of American identity resides in this very misconception, for one can dwell only by embracing the realm of the local where the corpse of the ethnic other lies buried. The Sioux chief Standing Bear explained the dilemma of American identity in similar terms:

> The white man does not understand the Indians for the simple reason that he does not understand America. The white man is too far from its formative processes. The roots of the tree of his life have not yet sunk down among the rocks of the soil.... The European is still a stranger; and he still hates the man who fought him step by step for this land. But in the Indian the spirit of the earth is still very much alive.... Many generations must pass before man can say that he truly belongs to a place; for this to happen, man's body must be shaped from the dust of his ancestors' bones.... Furthermore, by denying the Indians their rights and their ancestral heritage, the white men are only depriving themselves. (Hamilton 1950, Ital. tr., 1982: 300-1, 306).

Just as one must go through the surface of the map to read the map's history, so too must the American descend into the *«univers fractal»* of the local (Serres 1980b: 23) in order to dwell; but in so doing he inevitably calls down on himself the ethnic gaze. The Anglo-conformed version of American identity $(A+B+C=A)$ and the melting-pot version $(A+B+C=D)$ are both standard national formulas, abstract representations based on a primarily juridical and political definition the legitimacy of which derives from the nation-state (see Sollors 1981b: 277-81). As we have seen, the initial pluralism of native American tribes $(A+B+C=A+B+C)$ historically gave way to the above assimilationist identity patterns formulated during the process of national ethnogenesis and geographical expansion. Schematically speaking, it was during this process that the official, institutionalized, authoritative American typology affirmed itself as a strong subject, while the silenced, unofficial, delegitimized ethnic types were reduced to weak subjects. As my cartographic excursus has shown, however, the monocultural paradigm of identity is falsified in the very act of its self-verification.

«The Man That Was Used Up»

In Edgar Allan Poe's story «The Man That Was Used Up,» General John A.B.C. Smith---whose official identity can be formulated as $A+B+C=A$---has become a national hero by defeating the Bugaboo and Kickapoo Indians. Besides alluding to the Virginian colonist, whose dealings with the Indians are well known, «John Smith» is also the name of the American everyman. The drama of the story consists in the first person narrator's attempt to discover the mystery behind the General's physical perfection. In the scene of recognition the narrator finally learns that the hero's identity is a purely mechanical invention, not unlike Henry Adams's autobiographical manikin. Poe organizes the scene in such a way that the material construction of Smith's person, which is only made possible by the vigilant attendance of an old negro valet named Pompey, corresponds with the deconstruction of his personality. Smith is the American *citoyen* to the point of perfection: his identity is the product of his Indian conquests, of his suppression of the ethnic Other. The price he paid is revealed in the intertext from Corneille that follows the title: *«Pleurez, pleurez, mes yeux, et fondez vous en eau. / La moitié de ma vie a mis l'autre au tombeau.»* The other half in this case is actually the ethnic Other, since both strong subject and weak subject belong to a single stereoscopic structure. In burying the Indian, Smith buried half of himself.

Knowledge of American foundations, in other words, is built on a tomb. That is why the question of American identity must be asked in context, for without context there can be no answer. If, therefore, the identification of A involves a hermeneutical movement of dislocation from A to non-A, then American identity is best expressed as A(non-A). Ethnic difference, it should now be clear, is an intrinsic part of American identity; and since the non-A component has been removed---thus the parentheses of (non-A)---, the ethnic factor (our so-called weak subject) becomes an unknown. All this means is that the answer to Crèvecoeur's question is itself a questioning gaze. Without Pompey General John A.B.C. Smith would have no personality at all. Thus, the dominant identity patterns of $A+B+C=A$ and $A+B+C=D$ and the weak pattern of pluralistic ethnic anarchism, $A+B+C=A+B+C$, are merely internal versions of the basic relational structure A(non-A). When all is said and done, the ethnic self embedded in this costructuration can find expression only within the incorporated semiotic space of the United States.

In like manner, the American *citoyen* is definitionally tied to his own making, to an ethnogenetic quest that inevitably breaks up into such famous literary couples as Melville's Ishmael and Queequeg, Captain Delano and Babo, Cooper's Natty Bumpo and Chingachgook, Poe's Gordon Pym and Dirk Peters, Twain's Huck and Jim and the extraordinary twins of *Pudd'nhead Wilson,* and Faulkner's Isaac McCaslin and Sam Fathers. Americans are always on the move, their literature a literature of the road. As the script of American cultural geography teaches, the quest for identity and the search for a *patria* go hand in hand, as do the crisis of identity and the making of the map's surface.

But if the *logos* of the road creates continuity by canceling differences, a sense of place, and memory, the writing of the map cannot shake off its historical origins so simply. Every topological interpretation is also a diagram of the absent interpreter. Put in another way, cartographic kinesics---the act of interpretation that is inherent in the map---forces one to go through the map's fictional surface to its temporal structuring. The consequences of this unavoidable hermeneutical contortionism can also be seen in the literature of the road as the dominant model of American mainstream fiction. No matter where the American author finally chooses to strike through the pasteboard mask of American identity, his questing always brings him into contact with an ethnic subject, his other self. All told, these words of Deleuze and Guattari could easily be his: «My direct discourse is still the free indirect discourse that pierces me through and through, and that comes from other worlds or other planets» (1980: 107).

The culture of national unity and identity, which first produced the absolute voyage---the completely written voyage covering the face of the map---, is in turn now produced by the absolute voyager. Quest and identity crisis and circulation all amount to the same national program of seeing face to face. But the identity of the American nomad is structurally unstable not only because of his quest for the absolute voyage but also because the writing of this voyage can never really be completed. According to the law of entropy, absolute circulation, the making of the perfect map, is equivalent to total disorder and cartographic illegibility. Only by getting off the road and onto the chorographic map, only by seeing through a glass darkly, can entropy be avoided and the enigma of American identity faced.

CHAPTER THREE

WHAT IS THE ETHNIC?
A MODEL OF ETHNIC SEMIOSIS

«His words seemed detached, but they struck deep into Chalfonte. They were heavy with a thousand things unsaid, they bore the burden of a life and of a race. Behind them, as behind Black Hawk's immobile face, lay the tragedy that had overtaken his people, the destruction of all the aging chieftain had held close. His words were as a barrier between his race and the white man's race; more, he could not say, because he had said all; his words were primal and final....»
(from August Derleth's novel *Wind Over Wisconsin*).

«American people wonder at the tenacity with which the immigrant clings to the foods of his Fatherland. It is not strange, for the nostrils, the lips, the whole body retain precious memories of odours and tastes which are seldom forgotten.
I am inclined to believe that noodle soup, with the right kind of seasoning, touches more channels of memory than---say, a lullaby or even a picture of the homeland.»
(from Edward Steiner's autobiography *From Alien to Citizen*).

According to ethnic semiotics, in the beginning was the name. In order to discover who he is, in order to begin, the subject must interrogate the beginning of his name. Ethnic discourse is a discourse of foundations. «My name is Tsoai-talee. I am, therefore, Tsoai-talee; therefore I am,» Scott Momaday says in the opening page of his memoir *The Names;* and the storyteller who named him «believed that a man's life proceeds from his name, in the way that a river proceeds from its source» (1976). The foundations of ethnicity are based on the genealogical elaboration of the story behind one's name, one's family name. By discovering the self implicit in the surname, one produces an ethnic seeing and understands himself as a social, an ethnic, subject. Implicit in one's family name is a story of origins, a particular system of relations. As Pound says in Canto XCIX, the burden of sonship is «To trace out and to bind together» (1975: 695), which means the son, in order to be a son, must embrace a logic of deferment: by retelling the family story, he puts himself in touch with his origins. In other words, the system of relations making up the history of the family name is a dynamic system of ethnic recognition whose constructive matrices generate ethnic meaning. To speak of ethnicity, therefore, is to speak of ancestry, but as a pragmatic strategy of ethnic identification.

Due to the massive invasion of immigrants in the first decades of the twentieth century, melting-pot advocates and legislators insisted on an all-American type, while Ellis Island officials demanded a pronounceable name. In his description of «The Body of an American» in his novel *Nineteen Nineteen,* John Dos Passos named this «hundredpercent» representative self «John Doe,» with the added advice, «Make sure he ain't a dinge, boys. Make sure he ain't a guinea or a kike...» (1969, Vol. II: 462). F. Scott Fitzgerald's hero, who was part of John

Doe's war, showed he understood the rules of the game when he changed his name from James Gatz to Jay Gatsby, although his past still came back to haunt and defeat him. Indeed, with a name like Ludwig Lewisohn, one could not find a teaching position in the American university system at the beginning of this century (Lewisohn 1926: 173).

As the guardians of the national culture knew all too well, names are symbolic systems that unwittingly represent and reproduce multi-ethnic values. At any rate, in those early years it was a question of ideological procedure, of national circulation and defense. Evidence showed that those foreigners who looked backward instead of forward or sought their identity too passionately in natural bonds or blocked monocultural continuity by inhabiting the semantically chaotic urban ghettoes did not conform to the American program of *habitare*. Ethnic deferment was ultimately disruptive. In an attempt to march in step with the American Way, the majority of immigrants, blacks, and Indians were at least superficially willing to let go of their unique patrimony, as Maxine Hong Kingston explains in *The Woman Warrior:* «The Chinese I know hide their names; sojourners take new names when their lives change and guard their real names with silence» (1977: 5). Even those who were not so disposed seemed to create only a minor if not cryptic ethnic noise. The dominant culture, of course, went on whistling the same national tune and did not really bother about local otherness and ethnic difference. Its heroes, palimsests of a rather well-defined typological pantheon, continued to reproduce the American character. All told, it seemed that the assimilative process had succeeded quite well in defending the national culture and character, in melting the foreign residuum into an ideologically pure alloy.

A Land Full of Ghosts and Ethnic Signs

But the question James posed in 1904 was not really answered in the succeeding six decades, for even if one argues that ethnic groups as groups did not really speak out during these years, thus leaving the impression that they were quite Americanized, they still continued ever so ethnically to *see*. Speaking of her own group, the Chinese Americans, Maxine Kingston helps to explain the nature of this invisible presence when she notes, «What we have in common are the words at our backs» (1977: 53). Words spin a silent system of recognition and a unique point of view. Due to what she calls «Chinese-sight» (205), the author is able to see that far from being a country of the future, America is actually full of ghosts.

The problem here is one of understanding how a local semiotics, how an intensional theory of ethnic meaning embedded in the dominant culture, works. «What I'11 inherit someday is a green address book full of names,» Kingston says toward the end of her memoir (206); what she means is that there are stories within words, and within stories a hidden cultural identity. The whole process of ethnic seeing is as much an act of the imagination as it is an act of recovering lost origins. Thus, Momaday writes:

> Mammedaty was my grandfather, whom I never knew.
> Yet he came to be imagined posthumously in the going on of the blood, having invested the shadow of his presence in an object or a word, in his name above all. He enters into my dreams; he persists in his name. (26)

For anyone struck by the fact that against impossible odds the Indian did not vanish after the Dawes Act of 1887---or after he was finally and officially made an American citizen in 1924---, the name «Mammedaty» raises a disconcerting problem of cultural fluency.

All the while ethnic subjects were constantly and

quietly reinterpreting the official American sign according to local cultural needs, the global culture was merrily unaware of its own internal colonies, of its own graphic richness. More succinctly, it is not Jay Gatsby who ultimately calls the American Dream into question but James Gatz, whose story neither Fitzgerald nor his narrator, Nick Carraway, was capable of telling. A sign can only be identified when placed within its specific system of semiosis. But no matter in how elliptical or fragmented a way, the ethnic sign never ceased to circulate in the dominant cultural map and in mainstream narrative texts. The importance of this fact lies in the following ascertainment: as soon as one passes from the non-ethnic to the ethnic sign, he virtually undermines the entire homothetic continuum of American culture. The simple device of the name alone poses a rudimental crisis and opens up a semantic black hole, as Mark Helprin shows in his short story «Ellis Island»:

> Rabbi Koukafka had said that Jews were not wanted for manual labor. Furthermore, I had had outstanding luck as Guido da Montefeltro and as Hershey Moshelies. I thought that the unfamiliar tumult in which I found myself required an active defense, at least in the beginning, since, for me, America was a dreamworld. And I had customarily (perhaps habitually) been willing to do my share in the nurturing of confusions. Therefore, I thought for a while, and... arrived at a name for a heroic and dependable American worker.
>
> «Whiting Tatoon,» I said, staring toward the blue Pacific. (1982: 165).

In order to discover how ethnic sign production works, one must surrender to the kinesics of the ethnic stare, assume the ethnic point of view, and, as we shall see, go through the monocultural map. Helprin makes it clear that it is not the name but the strategy of the name that counts. Instead of affirming the principle of identity or non-contradiction, his protagonist opts for a strategy of con-fusion based on an underlying semiotic network of ethnic relations. In the light of the national program of *habitare* and the inevitable failure of its nomadic questing, difference can only be ethnic; the constructive dream of a unique American identity, only a deconstructive deferment of plural Otherness.

From Ethnic Fiction to Ethnic Semiosis

Ethnic fiction is ethnic to the extent that it produces ethnic semiosis and American fiction is hopelessly riddled with the ethnic sign. Both types of fiction belong to the same contextual dynamics of the relational structure discussed in the first chapter. Given the lack of reader competence in ethnic semiotics and the systematic neglect of the ubiquitous dissemination of the ethnic sign, it is useless to continue to discuss either mainstream or ethnic fiction in terms of form or primarily in terms of cultural encyclopedias. Since ethnic literary discourse is still fighting for cultural status, it is of crucial importance to clarify the type of complicity required by speaker and listener if they wish to communicate with each other.

Inserted as it necessarily is in a monocultural order and tradition of discourse, the ethnic sign is often intermittent, irregular, and weak. Unless one addresses it at this microstrategic level of performance, much of its critical potential will be lost. By emphasizing performance I am also suggesting more of a pragmatic than a semantic approach to the ethnic sign. Moreover, it is at the minimal level of the microstrategic that both micro- and macro-structural expressions of ethnic discourse can be seen to obey the same generative logic, that which is implicit in all semiotic activity: namely, the triadic relation of sign, object, and interpreter. Cultural fluency, in other words, must depend above all on the understanding of an inferencing activity that generates content rather than on an understanding of the ethnic contents themselves. While it is practically impossible to draw up an exhaustive inventory and taxonomy of an ethnic culture, and even armed with this encyclopedic expertise one is in no better position to control or predict ethnic sign production, it is more than possible to define the internal epistemology by which the subject continues to make and unmake himself as ethnic subject.

If, however, we are dealing with a model of a specific kind of semiotic activity which has its own comprehensive system of rules and its own grammar, so to speak, it is the subject and the subject alone who produces the model through a dynamic and contextual apprenticeship (Eco 1984: xi-xv; Borutti 1983: 111-28, 154-57). Granted, any general theory of ethnic semiosis and ethnic *savoir-faire* must ultimately be presented as a coherent formal elaboration capable of exhibiting its own structure and genesis. But this regulatory mechanism must not become reified or be taken as a static self-sustaining objectification. While the model makes ethnic discourse intelligible by showing the set of presuppositions on which ethnic strategies are based in the first place, it is the *ergon* of the subject that gives the model its fundamentally pragmatic and relational status. The rules of the model do not make sense outside of their application, and no set of rules can dictate how they should be applied in specific interpretative situations. Thus, the role of the subject cannot be eliminated; the model exists only for his sake, for the sake of identifying his concrete spatiotemporal acts. As James has already suggested, ethnic seeing cannot be separated from the seer, nor the seer from his act of seeing.

With this precautionary note, ethnic semiotics can now be defined as nothing more nor less than the interpretative gaze of the subject whose strategy of seeing is determined by the very ethno-symbolic space of the possible world he inhabits.[1] Implied here is a kind of double bind, because this model of seeing is conditioned by the following ethno-semiotic dynamics:

MEMORY $\longleftrightarrow$ PROJECT

Both the genealogical exercise that allows the subject to identify himself as ethnic and the imaginative act by which this subject produces an ethnic or multicultural project belong to the same interpretative circle. There can be no project without memory and without a project memory has neither coherence nor significance. The tensional structure between these two poles might be clarified further by Giulio Carlo Argan's remark, «Memory is experience that returns; imagination is the dreaming of experience» (1984: 4). Through the processing system of Memory and Project, the subject puts himself in contact with the foundational world of his ancestors, reproduces himself as member of an ethnic community, and is able to produce ethnic discourse.

A Politics of Memory

As a structural initiative, the questioning gaze of ethnic semiotics can be partially explained in terms of a politics of memory. In narrative discourse this search for roots takes the form of an extended mnemotechnical strategy whose rhetorical tropes are very closely monitored by a genealogical and topographical process which I have already called chorographic. The ethnic subject, in other words, goes through the national map in order to return to local origins. In Toni Morrison's novel *Song of Solomon,* for example, the Afro-American protagonist's genealogical quest leads him into the backwoods topography of Virginia:

87

In Roanoke, Petersburg, Culpeper he'd asked for a town named Charlemagne. Nobody knew. The coast some said. Tidewater. A valley town, said others. He ended up at an AAA office, and after a while they discovered it and its correct name: Shalimar. How do I get there?.... Buses go there? Trains? No.... He'd had to pay close attention to signs and landmarks, because Shalimar was not on the Texaco map he had.... Even at that, watching as carefully as he could, he wouldn't have known he had arrived if the fan belt hadn't broken again right in front of Solomon's General Store, which turned out to be the heart and soul of Shalimar, Virginia. (1978: 262-3).

While it does produce a poetics of recovery, this practice of return must not be mistaken for a pathetic anthropology, a nostalgic quest for what is irrevocably lost. No doubt there is a type of popular fiction based on a regressive ethnic poetics and I will discuss this later. What I want to focus on here is the perspectival mechanism behind the protagonist's quest and behind ethnic semiosis in general, as it is this which generates a radical interrogation of the authority of the official cultural scale. «For a long time now he knew that anything could appear to be something else, and probably was,» Morrison's narrator says of the protagonist (335), who eventually learns that one's interpretative gaze is only as long as one's ethnic memory:

He read the road signs with interest now, wondering what lay beneath the names. The Algonquins had named the territory he lived in Great Water, *michi gami*. How many dead lives and fading memories were buried in and beneath the names of the places in this country. Under the recorded names were other names just as «Macon Dead,» recorded for all time in some dusty file, hid from view the real names of people, places, and things. Names that had meaning... Names that bore witness. (333).

The protagonist then settles down to the task of

sonship, begins to discover «the real names,» and with these he weaves his generational story all the way back to Africa. Through this mnemotechnical strategy of recovery, the non-ethnic sign is radically transformed; that is, it becomes ethnic. As ethnic the subject now moves within the spiral of an originating project, thereby opening up a new hermeneutical space, a new stereoscopic competence, and a new type of semiotic performance. In fact, it is due precisely to the absence or opacity of the original ancestral *verbum* that ethnic reconstruction becomes necessary. Thus, the subject produces ethnic semiosis through a strategic use of memory which is nothing other than the topological and genealogical interrogation of the originating culture of his immigrant ancestors. In Morrison's text geography is a memory system while memory is geographical, and the ethnic protagonist very consciously organizes both of them genealogically. In other words, he goes forward by going backwards. It is this kind of questioning that produces an ethnic *savoir-faire,* both as competence and performance.

The new genealogical alignment produced through ethnic interpretation represents both a strategy of construction and a cultural construct, a pragmatic activity and a semantic system. If ethnic semiotic activity cannot but extend a semantic encyclopedia of ethnic data and leave behind what de Beaugrande and Dressler would call a long-term semantic memory (1981: 89), at the same time the conventional authority of the encyclopedia cannot but account for ethnic fluency, defining as it does the objective possibilities beyond which the ethnic sign cannot go without losing its ethnic distinctiveness. But, as a form of involuntary memory, the encyclopedia is without a subject. Only as a set of stored contextual usages or type-scenes, in which encyclopedic data are organized into narrative scripts by a subject, can there be a pragmatic and subject-oriented version of semantic production.

The distinction I want to make here is important because it means that the ethnic *traditio* itself must always be placed in the immediate processing context of Memory and ongoing Project. The Project interprets the ancestral world and the current ethnic encyclopedia as originating source; Memory understands them as originated fact. Consequently, the pragmatic and the semantic dimensions of the encyclopedia, its situational and conventional versions respectively, are indissolubly united in the activity of the subject, whose ethnic *habitare* is the frame, the spatio-temporal moment of ethnic semiosis. In ethnosemiotic framing both type-scene (properly the procedural sphere of the living ethnic community) and historico-anthropological system (properly the categorial sphere of intelligible and sensible systems) are relevant to the subject's inferencing field, while frame and encyclopedia are essential to ethnocultural reproduction. In other words, it is not a question here of the ethnic subject's living in the past but, as Sowell says (1981: 273), of the past living in him. The difference is one of means and ends. Within the context of a progressive ethnopoetics, the past is a means while the end is transgression of the national culture of *habitare*.

Two Versions of the Ethnic Encyclopedia

The above components of ethnic semiosis, with their emphasis on pragmatic performance, represent a further explicitness of my model and can be diagrammed as follows:

$$\text{FRAME} \longleftrightarrow \text{ENCYCLOPEDIA}$$

where Encyclopedia means both type-scene and cultural system. Thus, the cooperative circuit in which the subject is involved is actually triadic:

I will develop all these terms below; for the time being, it is more important to understand the crucial difference between a type-scene version of the encyclopedia and its logico-semantic system. As I have already demonstrated above, both dimensions are equally instrumental in generating an ethnic semiotics; indeed, they cannot be separated without seriously reducing ethnic sign complexity in specific narrative montages. It seems to me that the inherent shortcomings of many approaches to ethnic literature and ethnic discourse in general lie in the disproportionate emphasis given to the semantic component of the encyclopedia, an emphasis that can only break the triadic circuit to which it originally belongs. While an ethnic systematics may be necessary, in itself it is not sufficient. And, I would add, it is ultimately counterproductive, since any unilateral heuristic attempt to build a paradigm out of ethnicity ends in ghettoizing it.

Perhaps the critical triadic circuit which I consider indispensable to ethno-semiotic procedure can best be exemplified in this passage from John Cournos's novel *The Mask,* where the relation between competence and performance (between what is thought and actual thinking) are dramatically expressed:

> «A man's life,» observed Gombarov [the Jewish narrator]... «is on the surface a series of isolated pictures, yet in some mysterious way connected or grouped into a harmonious if not always a perfect pattern. And this invisible, continuous design, which runs through a man's life like a *motif* through a musical composition, is called character by some men, destiny by others....» Altogether this personality represented in its make-up a clash of races... a clash of reflective and energetic forces, and having been torn up by the

roots from its original mould, and replanted in another place, then reshuffled elsewhere---having, moreover, come under the influence of the unstable, shifting arts and moralities of the age, and yet kept something of the nature of its ancient soul---this personality was almost a physical symbol of the tenacious persistence of old spirits under the pressure of an age of iron, twentieth-century cosmopolitanism. (1919: 1, 5-6).

The «series of isolated pictures,» referring as they do to past events and an achieved patrimony, are fragments of an originated cultural encyclopedia, but as snapshots they are also irreducibly discontinuous moments lacking an explicit narrative context. The «clash of reflective and energetic forces,» on the other hand, is a depiction of the semiotic activity of the ethnic «personality,» whose «tenacious persistence» is responsible for weaving the fragments together. In turn, this «persistence» is ultimately due to the «invisible, continuous design» of the originating project of the ancestors. Yet the originating project, significantly, is not the static semantic version of the encyclopedia (the «original mould»), but the one made «visible» by the retrieving act of interpretation. In other words, there is no semantic encyclopedia without a pragmatic representation of it. If the encyclopedia accounts for ethnic difference, it is only by thinking differently that the subject constitutes himself as ethnic.

The very ability of the protagonist to stand between the dominant and the ethnic cultures and between the American present and the foundational past of the immigrant generation without losing his «ancient soul» suggests how time and space are redefined---not by the ethnic encyclopedia as such but by Gombarov's semiotic activity of reconstruction. The basic ethnic strategy here of cultural contrast and comparison implies a pragmatic *jeu* of shifting temporal dimensions in which the bare present is redeemed through genealogical enrichment. Time is released from its reductive *nunc* by means of ethno-semiotic framing, which combines both the tenses of Project and Memory. In this way the American crisis of *habitare* and identity is historicized through what now might be called the time of the ethnic frame. As for the space of the real, its naturalistic limits are exploded from within by the «clash» of an ethnic semiotics based on the frame/type-scene/cultural system triad.

It is this noetic circuit, and not any one of its single components, that transforms the monocultural space of «twentieth-century cosmopolitanism» into a polymorphic physiognomy of ethnic traces, associations, images, and symbols. Likewise, it is due to his genealogical recovery and interpretation of a meager handful of spatio-temporal ethnic fragments that the protagonist is in a position to see beyond the entropic conditions of national topology. This «seeing beyond» is possible because even the smallest fragment (here the snapshot), when read as a hermeneutical object, is itself placed semiotically outside of the culture of crisis. (Earlier I referred to this ethnic perspectivism as stereoscopic). With this new pragmatic definition of an ethnic *savoir-faire,* we now have an intensional, rather than merely extensional, going beyond or, as Cournos put it in the above passage, the insertion of a dialogical «clash» capable of redimensionalizing the spatio-temporal restrictions of the culture of the national map.

If one understands the cultural system of the ethnic encyclopedia as an activity, and this can be done by inserting it into the semiotic circuit of framing to which it naturally belongs, then he can capture the eruptive force of the single ethnic sign as well as all those micro-strategic fragments that float beyond the precise boundaries of a consolidated ethnic community with its evident semantic extension. But I will come back to the moment of the frame later; here it is the nature of the encyclopedia that is under examination.

While the cultural system of the encyclopedia represents a total organization of what is generally held to be true about an ethnic world (see de Beaugrande & Dressler: 89), it is still reductive to make this categorial knowledge normative in the evaluation of ethnic discourse, for the simple reason that this very primary matter does not allow one to explain ethnic frame activity or to predict how it will be organized narratively. What has already been thought has no pragmatic control over the ethnic subject's present thinking. Indeed, this version of the encyclopedia expresses the maximum distance possible between bare semantic data and a specific subject-oriented context.

Having said this, however, I do not wish to play down the unreplaceable role its intelligible and sensible systems have in a historico-anthropological analysis of ethnic semiosis. In his book *New Perspectives in Nonverbal Communication* Fernando Poyatos has convincingly shown how an inventory of these encyclopedic systems (which he breaks down further into human-somatic, objectual, environmental and animal systems as well as religious, societal, political, folkloric, and cultural systems) elaborates an interdisciplinary and metacommunicative competence that no other heuristic dimension of my semiotic triad can (1983: 337-68). Furthermore, none of the other components of my diagram reveal the broad extensional parameters and the stability of an ethnic culture.

In fact, only here can one locate the stored historical and traditional information which a casually chosen ethnic subject or author may not know or be in a position to discover. That is also why I chose earlier to call this dimension the realm of the ethnic subject's possibility and the ethnic group's collective memory. If ethnicity can be measured quantitatively, and to a certain extent it can, it is the descriptive potential of the encyclopedia that makes it possible; if an ethnic culture can be read as an institutional system, then it is the *auctoritas* of the encyclopedia that accounts for its cognitive coherence and continuity; if one can *a posteriori* form metadiscursive connections between scattered and ethnically contaminated narrative frames and between discontinuous ethnic sign chains, then it is the presuppositional structure implicit in the encyclopedia---considered as a possible world---that allows for it.

The Inevitable Ethnic Gaze

Certainly, an ethnic semiotics must also be able to build a conventional representation of an ethnic core culture, one that goes beyond the episodic depictions of individual narrative texts to provide a comprehensive codification of an ethnic world view. In effect, it is so natural for ethnic narrators to mimetically ransack their respective cultural warehouses that I am inclined to posit a single impulse intrinsically at work in all ethno-semiotic activity. Simply put, the intensional mechanism of the ethnic gaze naturally seeks to verify its cultural project in extensional terms, although given the imposing presence of a dominant standard of American dwelling, this is frequently impossible or impracticable. Going back to a point I made earlier, the very ineradicable nature of this impulse is due to the absent presence of the originating ancestral source, often literally canceled by the Americanization or nationalization of culture in the United States. As Black Elk once said:

> I did not know then how much was ended. When I look back now from this high hill of my old age, I can see the butchered women and children lying heaped and scattered all along the crooked gulch as plain as when I saw them with eyes still young.... A people's

dream died there. It was a beautiful dream.... the nation's hoop is broken and scattered. There is no center any longer, and the sacred tree is dead. (Brown 1972: 353).

But the problem is even more radical than what is implied in this historical act of scattering, important as it may be, because it is the inevitable absence of the original ancestral or immigrant *verbum* that demands and ultimately generates a continuous process of ethnic interpretation. In other words, the impulse to recover, rebuild, and maintain an ethnic *imago mundi* and an ethnic community is nothing but the genealogical principle itself. What is inherently radical about the ethnic subject's inability to change grandfathers, to put it in the classical terms of Horace Kallen's *Culture and Democracy,* is that he is unavoidably led to seek and elaborate upon the lost authority, the buried presence, of the original foundation. To believe that this is not a real ethnic imperative, one must close one's eyes to the perennial crisis of *habitare* within the juridical boundaries of the nation-state; but then the American quest for identity would belie disbelief.

In discourse terms, the intensional/extensional dynamics of the ethno-semiotic triad at the base of this discussion can be movingly exemplified by the speech Heinmot Tooyalaket (Chief Joseph) of the Nez-Percé Indians gave as he surrendered to General Bear Coat Miles in late September of 1887:

Tell General Howard I know his heart. What he told me before I have in my heart. I am tired of fighting. Our chiefs are killed. Looking Glass is dead. Toohoolhoolzote is dead. The old men are all dead. It is the young men who say yes or no. He who led on the young men [Ollokot] is dead.... My people, some of them, have run away to the hills, and have no blankets, no food; no one knows where they are---perhaps freezing to death. I want to have time to look for my children and see how many of them I can find. Maybe I shall find them among the dead. Hear me, my chiefs! I am

tired; my heart is sick and sad. Know where the sun
now stands I will fight no more forever. (Brown: 260)

What is described here is not only another scene
of ethnic scattering but also the genealogical desire,
expressed as Chief Joseph's search for his lost tribe, to
weave together once again the nation's broken hoop. The
conflict with the American government was originally
due to the forced removal of the Nez Percés, who were
given thirty days to transfer themselves and all their
worldly goods to a new reservation. Of course, Chief
Joseph had tried earlier to explain that «[T]he country
was made without lines of demarcation, and it is no man's
business to divide it» (Brown: 249); but he finally accepted the restrictions of the American scale map, the
reservation, after General Miles promised that what was
left of the tribe could return to its ancestral country. The
ethno-semiotic quest for origins, in other words, is also
a spatial and telluric preoccupation with extension. The
genealogical principle must be verified chorographically
as a local *habitare*. In the words of Heidegger, «Dwelling
consists in man's relation with places and, through places,
with space» (Norberg-Schulz: 23).

The difference between a strong and a weak cultural
system, between one that is highly elaborated and one
that is not, conditions the degree of authority it has in
ethnic sign production. The spatial schemes that allow
one to analyze its territorial sophistication are, in dimin-
ishing order, the following: world, region, city, quarter,
neighborhood, house, gesture, body (Vagaggini 1982:
167-68; Norberg-Schulz: 47). Surely one can read the
white man's advance and the Indian's dispossession as a
gradual impoverishing of the authority of an ethnic encyclopedia.

General Miles did not let Chief Joseph and his band
return to the Lapwai reservation in Idaho as he had
promised they could; instead, he shipped them to Fort

Leavenworth, Kansas, where their ethnic space was limited to gesture and body. If the others were finally permitted to return to Lapwai after many years, Chief Joseph was condemned to exile for the rest of his life. In the end, therefore, his ancestral culture was reduced for him to a mere desire, a mere *imago mundi*. Paradoxically, however, the very weakness of a cultural system can also show the contingent strength of ethnic semiosis: deterritorialized and, for all practical purposes, deprived of any material verification, the ethnic gaze can no longer be controlled, let alone measured or located. As Chief Joseph would have known, the gaze---the gaze alone---makes the near far and the far near, just as the presupposition of the gaze makes it possible to dwell and not the place of dwelling.

Type-scene Pragmatics

Perhaps the two major text types that rely heavily on the narrative strategy of elaborating a strong encyclopedia are the immigrant novel and autobiography, and it is certainly due to their use of a systematic *jeu* of anthropological extension that immigrant narratives also represent the legitimizing epicenter, the original authority, of ethnic literature as a whole. In the realm of discourse, however, the encyclopedia is pragmatically transformed and no longer remains a mere inventory of static data. Moreover, the ethno-semiotic triad of frame, type-scene, and cultural system has already suggested that the semantic version of the encyclopedia is part of a single heuristic circle. Since immigrant fiction is largely a pragmatic rehearsal of the encyclopedia, and since it is at the level of the type-scene that the ethnic cultural system is organized into a homogeneous series of dynamic procedures, perhaps I should further define this next component of the triadic diagram before discussing its use in narrative representations of the cultural system.

A type-scene is an instructional gestalt composed of a prefabricated script, a fixed amount of semantic data, and a specific set of role slices, actions, settings, and goals. Its semiotic activity tends to be hypercodified, which makes the type-scene definitionally strong and socially representative of ethnic cultural practice. In fact, the type-scene version of an ethnic cultural system offers a complete and standard pragmatics of ethnic content and its situational structures are homologically intracultural. Type-scene usage also verifies a correct topical understanding of semantic data, thereby providing local control centers for evaluating ethnic truth at the rhetorical-metaphorical level of discourse(Alter 1981;Goffman 1974; Eco 1984: 174-6). Because the type-scene is structured as a performance, its spatio-temporal organization is associated with typical capacities, events, and roles, embodies a specifically ethnic perspective, and reveals an ethno-semiotic interpretative calculus. With this definition of a type-scene in mind, we can now turn to the strategy of encyclopedic construction as exemplified in immigrant fiction, since any discussion of an ethnic world view must ultimately begin with the ancestors.

As Anthony Smith writes in his book *Ethnic Revival,* it is the myth of a common and distinct origin in time and space that is essential to the formation of a sense of ethnic community in that it marks the beginning of the history of the group and thus its individuality (115). In terms of the myth, of course, it is useless to try to separate encyclopedic origins from the quest for them. All gets confused in the ethno-semiotic gaze where subject and object become one. Among the best literary metaphors for expressing this unconditional confusion is the immigrant chest in Ole Rölvaag's novel *Giants in the Earth,* which represents the cultural patrimony and the original belongings of the Holms, a Norwegian immigrant family that settled in the Dakotas when these states were still a territory. The chest had originally belonged to Beret Holm's great-grandfather and represents for her all that remains of her old-world culture in the United States. In the course of the novel it becomes a focal point around which significant ethnic events are organized, and this to the extent that it becomes the dominant image of a bound cultural encyclopedia. When the parents die, their cultural inheritance is passed on to the children; only now they must practice a politics of memory in order to piece together the original patrimony. After the death of the ancestors, the founding ethnic *verbum* is lost and ethnic interpretation as a Memory←→Project dynamics begins.

In the immigrant novel the ancestors, the fathers and mothers, dominate. Their story is governed by a foundational project (implicit in the act of emigration/ immigration) or by the projection of a possible world. The idea is to begin life over again. In Part Two, «Home-founding,» of *Giants in the Earth,* Rölvaag expresses the theme of encyclopedic construction this way:

> The talk had now drifted to questions of a more serious nature, mostly concerned with how they should manage things out here; of their immediate prospects; of what the future might hold in store for them; of land and crops, and of the new kingdom which they were about to found.... No one put the thoughts into words, but they all felt it strongly; now they had gone back to the very beginning of things.... (1927: 32).

As this type-scene passage suggests, the narrative logic of encyclopedia building involves both a competence and a performance and these are necessary to reproduce a material cultural system. The thematic roles of the protagonists are almost exclusively scripted as a single process of ethnic founding, as an authoritative act of elaborating a local cultural territory. As Vilhelm Moberg says in the preface to the third volume of his tetralogy, *The Settlers,* «He [the immigrant] had come to make a living for himself and his family, he must build a house and establish a home; he must build up a new society from its very foundation» (1961: 9). There is in this passage, and in ethno-semiotic constructive activity as a whole, a self-conscious sense that the immigrant undertaking is a mythological or epic exploit, that it is a history-making act.

Indeed, through their topological movement from one country to another, which is ordered narratologically according to the motif of the journey, the emigrants tend to project their conception of ethnocultural space as a homogeneous ideal habitat. The utopian impulse of the protagonists and their clarity of vision also help to create this type of strong encyclopedic space, as is evident in this type-scene from John Cournos's novel *The Mask:*

> It was settled that they should go to the new land of milk and honey. But where? What city? Again Vanya came with the suggestion. He read aloud from his geography book: «Philadelphia, 'the city of brotherly love,' is celebrated for its public institutions, its hospitals, its schools, its free colleges of learning.».... like children they all believed implicitly the words in the geography book. (102-3).

The protagonists (above all the fathers) cannot help but take on a certain heroic stature in such a context, and their Homeric potentiality is often confirmed not so much by their actions as by the fact that these are frequently communal (see Rölvaag's Norwegians, Moberg's Swedes, Pietro Di Donato's Italians, August Derleth's Germans). At any rate, in the task of encyclopedic construction, doing tends to dominate over thinking, for, in Peter Grimsen's words in Sophus Keith Winther's novel *Take All to Nebraska,* «There was scope for action here» (1936: 279). With construction as the master topic, goals are still relatively uncomplicated, cultural motives are few, simple, public in character, and usually agreed upon by all. The ethnic project inspires consensus, and consensus inspires the building of an ethnic community. Structural cooperation is expressed as a cultural-psychological mobilization within the group itself, whereby it ideologizes its own ethnic culture to the point of transforming it into a model (Rothschild: 61).

Thus, even such a spatial scheme as the black ghetto, usually considered a non-place (a place that blocks circulation) by the dominant white culture, can become a positive encyclopedic territory, as Maya Angelou shows in her autobiography *I Know Why The Caged Bird Sings:*

> The beautiful buildings sat on a moderate hill in the white residential district, some sixty blocks from the Negro neighborhood. For the first semester, I was one of three Black students in the school, and in that rarefied atmosphere I came to love my people more. Mornings as the streetcar traversed my ghetto I experienced a mixture of dread and trauma. I knew that all too soon we would be out of my familiar setting, and Blacks who were on the streetcar when I got on would all be gone and I alone would face the forty blocks of neat streets, smooth lawns, white houses and rich children.
> In the evenings on the way home the sensations were joy, anticipation and relief at the first sign which said BARBECUE or DO DROP INN or HOME COOKING or at the first brown faces on the streets. I recognized that I was again in my country.(1978: 182).

Encyclopedic extension here is like an amniotic fluid. Angelou seems to imply that no person can lose his/her chorographic map and still hope to keep a sense of ethnic identity intact. Both ethnic gaze and identity derive from the same local source, and, according to the semiotic circuit of frame, type-scene, and cultural system, it would be irrelevant to try to say which is responsible for cultural continuity. Encyclopedic foundations do fade away into myth and the ethnic genealogical strategy is a *mise en abîme*.

The Making of Popular Ethnic Fiction

Even so, there is a significant aesthetic difference between the revivalist strategies of encyclopedic extension used by popular fiction and those employed by such serious ethnic expressions as the immigrant novel and autobiography. Popular ethnic fiction is almost exclusively a fiction of type-scenes; that is, it simply revives a traditional set of ethnic themes, subjects and situations. Since it literally overdevelops or overextends the ethnic encyclopedia, it is mostly concerned with cultural reproduction rather than semiotic production; with rehearsal rather than with the rekeying of ethnic meaning according to contemporary needs. The ethnic protagonist is almost entirely spoken by encyclopedic elaboration and can be said to be a mere structural effect of it. In short, he adds nothing new to the ethnic cultural system, his function being that of confirming what has already been established. Umberto Eco would call this revivalist tactic a *ratio facilis* (1984: 43) because its discourse is preformed, its semiotic activity above all commemorative.

This means that its narrative logic is for the most part committed to a *jeu* of equivalences so that it risks very little in terms of serious intercultural contact. In fact, such popular fiction often acts as if the cultural imperatives of the national state did not exist, did not threaten or challenge local ethnic models. Of course, even such intercultural conflict can be considered as within its scope if it is stereotypically handled. But these automatisms read like a replay of presumably fixed and static situations, to the point that the reader may even forget that the cultural dynamics being described are really historical and not ritualistic.

In serious ethnic fiction, however, the ethnic sign is not so socially fixed or predictable because its very position within the culture of the national map makes it peremptorily unstable. In comparison, the ethnic sign of popular fiction is only apparently relational, since it does not risk calling into question its own status by venturing beyond the encyclopedic parameters originally established by the foundational efforts of the ancestors. Novels like Rölvaag's or even Winther's, both historical novels, engage the dominant culture head on in the very process of unfolding an ethnic gestalt, thereby jeopardizing the success of the ethnic project from the start.

Here the goal is interpretation of the past and not the past itself. In fact, it is by means of the attempt to renaturalize the scale map in the context of the past that ethnic semiosis is capable of producing new interpretation in the present. Through this intensional dynamics of ethnic sign production, ethnic fiction is indeed a significant contemporary performance. Far from being a mere archeological exercise in the quest for origins and natural bonding, serious ethnic semiosis claims the right to redefine the boundaries of ethnic interaction and the place of ethnicity in American culture. This, then, is the type of inferencing field that offers the proper theoretical conditions for thinking ethnically in practice and my local model of ethnic semiosis is intended to define and defend only the kind of ethnic interpretation that can also be found in the smallest sign frame.

Before taking up the last component of the triadic circuit of my diagram, namely the frame, I would like to make a few concluding remarks about type-scene pragmatics as exemplified in immigrant fiction. It is primarily with the activation of narrative elements from this type of text that a rather detailed map of an immigrant/ethnic world view is charted: a stock of themes, characters, actions, situations, objects, customs, beliefs, institutions, and so forth---all of which establish a bound cultural encyclopedia. A good part of the epistemological space of this type-scene construct is taken up with the perspectival focus of the ancestors or immigrants, and if this is not so, there is at least a strong sense of genealogical orientation and cultural continuity often clearly rooted in an old-world reality. But what makes the originating cultural encyclopedia strong is not the fact that the story of foundations begins in «the world of our fathers,» to use the words which Irving Howe chose as the title of one of his books, but the fact that it is bound by an ethnic community actively involved in a living cultural enterprise.

In short, it itself is a world, even if its actual space is a rather tightly restricted ghetto or reservation. The individual ethnic subject is still part of a family, and the family part of a homogeneous community. There is a network of preeminently intracultural relations. It is this ongoing originating world that germinates an ethnic semiosis based on strong sign chains. Here social identity is mediated by a broad context of ethnic referentiality, although in the final count everything still depends on the sons and daughters. In most circumstances, in fact, this means that ethnic interpretation lives and dies with the single subject and his or her ethnic gaze.

A Semiotics of Ethnic Framing

Situational ethnicity, a weak version of ethnic identity, involves a semiotics of framing. While there is a reasonably definable encyclopedic core to every ethnic culture, it is theoretically impossible to define its intensional limits. As long as there is an ethnic subject, any object can function as ethnic even in a non-ethnic context.

Likewise, any sign can be read as ethnic if it is placed within an ethnic sign system. In other words, there is no limit to what can be put into ethnic relation. It is simply a question of semiotic *kinesis,* as James already knew in 1904.

Of course, it would be easy to dismiss the fleeting ethnic glance as ineffectual, as a weak epistemology incapable of producing its own world view. Daniel Fuchs and John Cournos might even be cited here as supporting evidence insofar as they casually refer to this marginal cognition as a praxis of *zakhar* (remembering) or, in the words of Fuchs, as a mere game of old men who «play tick-tack-toe with the great Talmud»:

> old men who find synagogues in a tenement basement store with the terrible toilets facing the back yards. These old men nodding over the yellow, holy-odored volumes, arguing in a straight line of tradition that extends over the world in width, in depth to the earliest times, in length to God himself. (1961: 51).

But it is this very «weakness» that generates a new subversive here/elsewhere, a unique ethno-semiotic space that breaks down all cultural limits by its interpretative nomadism. Cournos, for example, admits that his protagonist, Gombarov, is a misfit, a wandering Jew (in *Babel* 1922: 385), but he also admits that the long life of his people runs through him like «a mystic force, a living fluid running down the spine» (in *The Mask* 1919: 31). Fuchs's protagonists, on the other hand, decide finally to remain schlemiels and stubbornly refuse to accept the moral degradation of ghetto conditions. In the end they remain in Williamsburg, but they do not «dumbly submit» (247).

The principal task of the sons and daughters in ethnic fiction is to reinterpret the status of the referent as defined by the ancestors. This involves putting contemporary reality between the parentheses of Project and

Memory, so that its time and space become a false floor which gives way to the free-falling ethnic space of Rölvaag's novel *Their Fathers' God* (1931). The parameters of this world are indeed elusive and fluctuating, for at any moment and in any place traces of it may uncontrollably and involuntarily reappear in a face, an accent, an object, a gesture. With the disestablishment of the originated world of the ancestors, the *traditio* may be deterritorialized, may no longer be clearly signified (except as a product of quotation, stereotyping, anthropology, archeology). But in this case the *traditio* itself now becomes the hermeneutical object, the signifying source that makes the difference.

If the problem of cultural continuity becomes critical in the presence of a weak or unbound ethnic encyclopedia, ethnic semiosis is still possible through the floating practice of an ethnic *savoir-faire*. Ethnic fiction, in other words, can be classified as such to the extent that it *produces* ethnic interpretation in new ways, to the extent that the interpreting protagonist produces a positive strategy of perspectival contrast and comparison by means of a genealogical interrogation of his/her *traditio*. This type of framing can be weak or strong, passive or active, involuntary or voluntary, discontinuous or continuous, floating or spatially located in an ethnic community. Ethnic interpretation can be a starting point in fiction or a point of arrival, as it is in Rölvaag's *Their Fathers' God,* where in the very last lines of the novel there is a radical reappropriation of ethnic seeing by Peder, the protagonist---whose mixed marriage has just gone on the rocks:

> And going to the corner back of the door he began hunting among the clothes that hung there, aimlessly and with slow movements.
> «Looking for something?» asked Jacob Fredrik.
> «That old cap of mine,» he answered, absently,

> and continued turning the clothes.... «What time did she leave?»
>
> «This morning, shortly after I came down,» gulped Jacob Fredrik.
>
> Peder found the cap, which all the time had hung in plain sight, put it on, and went out. (338).

The novel ends here. The act of putting on his old cap (ironically «in plain sight»), while not offering a new transparency or an end to the protagonist's problems, does suggest a new perspectival commitment, a hermeneutical return to his old Norwegian ways. Granted, Peder simply «went out»; we do not know where. But we do know with what competence, it seems to me. Rölvaag's open ending indicates that the semiotic space of ethnic fiction is now everywhere and nowhere at the same time: everywhere because Peder's going out is topologically unlimited; nowhere because his ethnic perspective is based on the absent presence of the hieroglyphic gaze of his dead father iconically framed in the closing scene of *Giants in the Earth*. Thus, through Peder's role as ethnic semiotician this nowhere becomes a cultural everywhere. As the Norwegian minister warns his people in *Their Fathers' God*, «A people that has lost its traditions is doomed» (207), but Peder adds:

> It would be folly to try to build up the different European nations over here. The foundation is new, the whole structure must be new, and so it shall be. (210).

Of course, Peder and not the minister is right in affirming that ethnic reconstruction is not so much a repetition as it is a dialogical production. Ethnic semiotics is *about* genealogy precisely because it produces a poetics of continuity through the current act of interrogating the world of the ancestors.

The ethnic narrative program, with its perspectival *jeu,* is very much a reinterpretation of the *traditio* elaborated as a homological cultural encyclopedia. While the latter is the best semantic/pragmatic apparatus we have for verifying the degree to which a given ethnic culture is metanarratively embedded in a particular text, only the situational semiotic activity of the protagonist as ethnic interpreter can reveal how this encyclopedic material is recovered and put to use in new ways. A work of fiction invests in ethnicity to the extent that it is stocked with various ethnic *savoirs* selected from the encyclopedia, but the type of selections and the degree of their expansion, distribution, and narrative significance are equally important.

Indeed, the encyclopedia itself may lack the intrinsic ordering principle (an institutional and communal authority) capable of organizing its complexity into a totality. It may be without a binding or a center, largely virtual and present only as a series of mobile and free-floating sign sequences. In this sense, much ethnic fiction is epistemologically weak but, it bears repeating, this can also become its peculiar semiotic strength. Ethnicity may now be only optional and symbolic, a micro-strategic and rhizomatic device (Deleuze & Guattari 1980: 9-37) of double awareness which has no desire to retotalize a buried encyclopedia but which also has no desire to abandon the practice of ethnic semiosis.

The ethnic self, therefore, may choose either to develop a local cultural map or float about in the dominant culture as exegete or interpreter of the ethnic traces inscribed everywhere (but nowhere) in the American topology. According to this strategy, ethnic semiotics is nothing but the interpretation of the genealogical history that the ethnic perspective produces. This type of semiosis, the result of a radical discontinuity between the ethnic American self and his *traditio,* is the very story of a cultural difference; not only the story of an ethnic perspective but more importantly the story of its genealogical reconstruction.

Now my semiotic triad can be completed, for within the context I have just described even the constructed material of the extended encyclopedia is seen to be of zero sign value if not put in an ethnic relational structure, if not filtered by a framing subject. It is not only a matter of unilaterally rehistoricizing the world of the ancestors, therefore, since it is even more important that the besieged ethnic subject learn to function ethnically in the dominant culture. He cannot but dwell in the conjunctural *hic et nunc* where intercultural performance is all, where the encyclopedia is only useful insofar as it helps the subject to experiment with and reinvent ethnicity *in situ*. This radically situational moment of contact is the moment of the ethnic frame, of ethnic subjectivity and ethnic speech, and represents the most dynamic and volatile level of the semiotic triad as well as the most current, even if episodic, version of the encyclopedia. Through frame pragmatics the subject constantly produces new perspectives of the encyclopedia, constantly tests its relevance and stability. By dwelling in the frame, the ethnic subject is forced to question encyclopedic foundations and penetrate ever more deeply into its core until, finally, its center and circumference are one. Compared to the centripetal force of the type-scene, therefore, the frame is restlessly centrifugal. Nor could it be otherwise, tied as it is to the moment of encounter where the uniqueness and accidental structure of experience make it impossible to say what will happen.

In fact, any attempt to codify the basically idiosyncratic context of the frame by inserting it in the recurrent pragmatics of the type-scene can only result in the erasing of the specific and fleeting significance of the frame itself. If the type-scene is thought at rest, then the frame is thought in action (Miceli 1982: 603, 605); if the encyclopedia's function is to moderate ethnic meaning, then the frame's is to modify it. Instead of trafficking in types, thereby reconfirming the established field of ethnic identity through repetition, the frame proposes actorial roles never evident until then, thus introducing an ethnic *novum* unrepeatable in time and space. It is this fundamentally contractual or dialogical dimension that makes it impossible to explain or predict frame genesis by means of encyclopedic description. Between the semantic stasis of the latter and the pragmatic action of the former there is a qualitative leap.

Due to the often contradictory praxis of frame semiotics and the frequently opaque relationship between frame and encyclopedia, it is not unusual for ethnic sign production to take the form of what Umberto Eco would call a *ratio difficilis* (1984: 43). For if at the level of the type-scene the ethnic self is a subject of the encyclopedia, at the level of the frame he both is and is not. That is, in context he is often an inter-subject, one who may choose to identify positively with his ethnic cultural system or simply express it as the unknown difference that allows him to criticize the dominant culture to which he undeniably belongs. In this last instance, the frame is ethnically weak and the ethnic factor quite uncontrollable. The ethnic sign merely indicates a difference, a «non-A» that must ultimately be discovered if one hopes to understand how ethnic semiotics functions as an absent presence or as a mere act of dissimilation. On the other hand, in order for the interpretative gaze of the subject to be ethnic, there must also be at least an implicit relation between the subject and his cultural encyclopedia or there can be no ethnic framing at all. What we have, in other words, is a semiotic circuit with its own internal coherence, its own system of pertinence, and its own heuristic apparatus. This ethnic *habitare* can now be summed up in the following, completed diagram:

111

MEMORY   FRAME

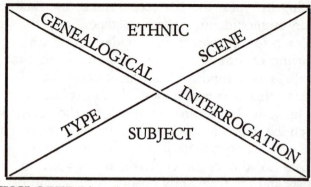

ENCYCLOPEDIA   PROJECT

    While the vertical axis of MEMORY and ENCY-
CLOPEDIA illustrates the collective level of the ethnic
community and the world of the ancestors, the parallel
axis of FRAME and PROJECT stands for the idiosyncratic
level of the individual subject. The diagonal line of
ENCYCLOPEDIA, TYPE - SCENE, and FRAME (a
procedural apparatus for analyzing the process of cultural
storage and activation) explains the cooperative relation
between the semantic and pragmatic dimensions of
my model. The other diagonal line---MEMORY and
PROJECT---represents the semiotic activity of genealogical ordering and interrogation that defines the unique
inferencing field of the ethnic subject. By moving from
MEMORY to PROJECT, the self becomes a thinking
subject; by moving in the reverse direction, he identifies
with what has already been thought. The former is an
innovative act, the latter conservative. But if this is the
grammar, the set of rules, by which sign production
becomes ethnic, it is only in context that its structural
implications can be understood. In any account, the
hypothetical subject at the center of the diagram remains
simply a ghost if not given a local habitation and a name.

Perhaps one of the best and most transparent literary *topoi* for examining how the above grammar functions in the *faire-être* of the ethnic subject is the feast, the ethnic group gathering; for, paradoxically enough, few communicational formats are as rigidly codified and governed by such rudimentary narrative structures and yet capable of opening up so many intimate and unexpected adventures in ethnocultural exploration. Quite frankly, there are few moments like the ethnic feast where ethnic identity can be so positively affirmed and socially reinforced (see Greimas 1983: 160ff).

The scene itself already presumes a considerable amount of cultural construction as well as the fulfillment of this prophecy by Isaiah (65: 21): «And they shall build houses, and inhabit them; and they shall plant vineyards, and eat the fruit of them.» The banquet rests on ritual foundations and is an institutional act of celebration. In his book *Americans by Choice,* made up of seven autobiographical stories, Angelo Pellegrini writes:

> There are feasts in every story. There are even recipes.
> There is discussion of wines.... All of these are basic
> values. (1956: 4).

Indeed, it would not be farfetched to say that without recipes there could be no feast and that both competence and performance are held together by the shared ethnic values that circulate in both. By seeing how one passes from raw ingredients to the act of eating and enjoying a fully prepared meal, by seeing how an ethnic feast functions, we will also be able to learn how the grammatical systematics of ethnic semiosis is transformed into an act of contextual application. And if the generative program of the recipe will be our basic focus, the Italian Americans will be our ethnic agents.

Before the process of transformation can begin, the cook must already have a stock of information and materials at his/her disposition. In this case the garden is our metaphor for the ethnic encyclopedia, since it appropriately contains the as yet unassembled raw data that will eventually become an aromatic dish. Although in their natural state these materials present a rather elementary and unselected horticultural array, they are still a powerful locus of ethnic binding and already delineate the possibilities and limits within which the cook will have to work. It is truly surprising how frequently the garden appears in Italian-American narratives---from the spice garden of Marietta Simone (with its *basilico, finòcchio*, Italian parsley, and leaf-chicory) in Jo Pagano's novel *Golden Wedding* (1943) to Rosario's garden of basil, sage, chives, garlic, and peppers in Joe Vergara's autobiography *Love and Pasta* (1968)---, but perhaps no Italian-American text illustrates its symbolic potential as well as Pellegrini's:

> She smiled as she surveyed the straight rows and the rich black earth that she had tilled for so many years; for she knew the children would come.... And she knew, too, that they would come frequently and unannounced because there was a bond between them and herself and the little plot of earth that had been their first home in America. (7).

While the time and place of the feast are virtually dependent on the semantics of the garden, culinary performance is very much a pragmatic matter of apprenticeship, of learning the typical ways of making various kinds of herbs and vegetables ethnically palatable. The mere mention of the script «Italian feast,» whether the occasion be a picnic, a birthday party, a wedding or a saint's day celebration, immediately suggests not only a rather predictable set of types, actions and themes, but also a conventionally organized *abbuffata* (euphemistically, a banquet) of ravioli, spaghetti and sauce, chicken *alla cacciatora,* stuffed peppers and artichokes, various kinds of roasts, spicy sausage, salads, mushrooms, olives, cheese, fried pastries, and, to wash it all down, homemade wine. «But on Sundays and holidays it was assumed that your appetite became gargantuan and, besides soup and salad, you were expected to stow away at least three different courses of meat, four or five vegetables, along with celery and fennel, all topped off with pastry, fruits, and nuts,» Jerre Mangione writes in *Mount Allegro* (1942: 136).

The subsystems of ethnic know-how implicit in the feast are incredibly rich and invariably a major topic of table discussion, for if all the participants know more or less what to expect seated, nobody really knows the peculiar technical twists that make everything special. Take wine-making and the trick of getting the polenta just right in Mari Tomasi's novel *Like Lesser Gods* (1949) or the «secret formula for making alcohol out of the grape stems» (37) and the art of making *cannoli* in *Mount Allegro* or even the special way of shaping *fusilli* and *gnocchi* in Vergara's *Love and Pasta.* Apprenticeship clearly entails a representative symbolic perspective of food, a common store of ethnic wisdom, maxims, and folklore, not to speak of a shared cultural passion. As Mangione points out in his autobiography cited above, «Ordinarily, of course, a meal was more than a meal; it was a ritual...» (18).

The competence of the recipe, in other words, gives way to a larger performance in which the group itself becomes the protagonist. Just as the raw ingredients of the garden are transformed from one state into another through the recipe, so are the actual time and place of the feast transformed into a utopian space of ethnic identity through a genealogical exercise of storytelling, music, and group recollection. Pietro Di Donato writes in *Christ in Concrete,* «Five hours had they been at table and now they sat back and in the strong tobacco clouds that nearly obscured gaslight they talked of other days» (1939: 248). This much of the script is socially fixed. The feast generically functions as an act of historical synthesis in which each participant feels integrated into the semiotic space of his ethnic culture. In the ritual time of celebration the sense of community prevails and for the moment encyclopedia and subjective framing are strictly joined. As Jo Pagano writes in *Golden Wedding:*

> I recall the animated faces of the guests as they listened to it [the music], the sparkling recognition in their eyes, the sudden uncontrollable nods of their heads.... *Italia, Italia*---it was here in this room, compelling and unforgettable, the ancient soil which they, aliens in a foreign land, could neither deny nor yet forget completely---the Italy of their childhood, motherland, home, source of all their deepest memories and deepest desires.... (86).

Beyond this conventional level of the type-scene, however, there is also the specific frame context within which the time of celebration takes place. The feast cannot only be rehearsed but also rekeyed in many different ways, often depending on the state of intercultural relations at that particular moment. The feast, in other words, can be put to various *ad hoc* uses. In Vergara's autobiography Rosario takes his children to eat *capozzelli* at the San Gennaro festival in order to teach them about the role of festivals in Calabria, later on noting «the strange blindness of the great American nation where the best of everything was available and the people were content with tasteless food» (39). In *Mount Allegro* a picnic in the park next to an American family becomes an occasion of cultural contrast between the Italian (here Sicilian) and the American Way of life, while Pagano uses the feast simply to celebrate and recall an Italian couple's fifty years of ups and downs in America.

116

In each instance, the distinct narrative embedding of the feast gives it a different pragmatic function and purpose, even if all of the above examples follow the same constructive program and reveal remarkably similar behavioral repertoires, topics, and objectual inventories. A rather clearly circumscribed ethno-semiotic activity, the feast still succeeds in showing how the broad epistemological style of an ethnic group and the situational interpretation of it pertain to the same mode of seeing. Grammar and context are both complementary and inseparable; ethnic sign production is ultimately an encyclopedia/frame circuit. Only in the contingent flicker of the momentaneous frame, however, can the weakest ethnic sign be grasped, and at this level American literature itself becomes a vast capillary network in which the crisis of *habitare,* the crisis of the sons and daughters of an immigrant nation, is peremptorily ethnic.

CHAPTER FOUR

AN IRREVERENT POSTSCRIPT, ETHNIC DISCOURSE IN A POSTMODERN CONTEXT

«During my vigils, I went around the
mappemonde without finding rest.
(Me being absent, only the mappemonde
is real.)»
(from *Le Livre des Questions* by Edmond Jabès)

«History, ultimately, is not
the devastating bulldozer it is said to be.
It leaves underpasses, crypts, holes
and hiding places. There are those who survive.»
(from «La storia» by Eugenio Montale)

The preceding chapters were meant to show that
the culture of the national map and of American identity
is built on a half-truth. In order to see the whole truth,
one must go through the mirror and beyond the homological and isotropic continuum of federal space, for the
terms «American» and «ethnic» are themselves part of
a single relational structure. If, however, they express
two radically different ways of seeing and doing within
the same political boundaries, the problem of *habitare*
is the same for both of them. There are strangers in the
land, and I am referring not only to the hundreds upon
hundreds of thousands of new immigrants but also to

the citizens themselves. There are strangers in the land because of the spatial program of the national map. Everybody is officially on the road, looking for a better place to live.

At the beginning of his *U.S.A.* trilogy, Dos Passos's representative American youth is setting out on an adventure, starting out on a journey that will never end. The verbs identifying this conventional self are those of «searching,» «wanting,» «hoping,» and «contact.» But when he is engulfed by the urban crowd and by its primarily twentieth-century verbs («pack,» «climb,» «scamper,» and «filter»), he is essentially alone: he «walks by himself, fast but not fast enough, far but not far enough....» Eventually, he finds himself in a nocturnal, Poesque milieu with his «head swimming with wants.» This condition the narrator expresses as «No job, no woman, no house, no city.» The youth's quest suggests a sense not of possession but dispossession. He passes from active protagonist to passive witness, from the modality of wishing to that of mere «hearing» (Dos Passos 1969, Vol. 1: xix-xx). In both instances, however, the basic strategy remains the same. As William Carlos Williams counsels in his *Autobiography,* «[G]et on with it, keep moving, keep in, speed the nerves, their speed, the perceptions, theirs, the acts, the split-second acts, the whole business, keep it moving as fast as you can, citizen» (1967: 330). As a place, America does not exist; place has become process. The quest for a dwelling is now the crisis of *habitare,* and within this context the status of the self, the object, and the human-built environment is radically transformed. If Dos Passos's American and essentially Whitmanian youth falls back on the speech of the people at the beginning of the *U.S.A.* trilogy, by the end of his journey across the American habitat, it is the very status of the word that is undermined.

Being inside the crisis of dwelling, ethnic discourse

cannot but redefine its own possibilities, construct a practice appropriate to a new understanding of its own politics and art, and interpret its characteristic version of American facts in the light of the above epistemic shift. This new ethnic pragmatics, in order to preserve its critical function, will have to take into account a more perfected cartographic absence now organized on a technotronic and teletronic global scale; and in the very act of reflecting on its own limits, will discover the very strategies that make the ethnic *verbum* a major filter for reading the modern and so-called postmodern experience, not as a universal condition but as a historical construct. But by reconsidering the epistemological status of the categories of ethnic semiosis (origins, genealogical interrogation, memory, local place, and project), the ethnic subject must inevitably define ethnicity as a means and not an end. After all, the ancestors are dead, and in place of the real world there is now only a global strategy of possible worlds. The issue, therefore, is not ethnicity *per se* but the *uses* of ethnicity in a postindustrial society. This distinction is crucial, for it suggests what the nature of the ethnic sign now is. In the postmodern context, ethnic discourse can only be discourse about ethnic discourse or, if you will, a pseudo-discourse. What might be perceived here as a radical weakness in the performative potential of ethnic interpretation, however, is really, at second glance, its main strength. In order to demonstrate that this is so, it will be necessary to approach the larger issue of *habitare* in genetic terms.

The Crisis of Habitare

The new status of the ethnic *verbum* is the direct result of the larger crisis of *habitare* that characterizes the modernist condition. The cultural shift alluded to here can be summed up as the passage from the traditional city (the polis) to the city of *techné,* the metropolis. As Karl Scheffler wrote in 1913 in his book *The Metropolis:*

> America, this gigantic European colony, this truly modern country of commerce and industry, has today necessarily become the state of the metropolis. The difference between the past and the present consists in the fact that at first the metropolis was an exception, whereas today, both in the industrialized European states and in America, it has become typical. (Cacciari 1973: 167).

It is this new and above all American reality that has brought about a semantic catastrophe in the traditional ways of perceiving the self, objects, and the habitat in general. In her book *Spazio e immaginario* Paola Coppola Pignatelli notes, «The city is the reflection of a way of being and seeing the world» (1982: 138, plate 33). One could be even more emphatic and assert that human beings cannot do without relatively stable topological systems and that in their absence it is impossible to find a dwelling.

The metropolis is the perfect dynamic representation of the form of modern life. Its structure implies a world view; indeed, *forma urbis* and the modern *forma mentis* are homological. As we have already seen, the American ideology of conquest is essentially an urban myth and its linearity can be read in the making of the American map. The national map ultimately represents a total field of action, a network of lines in movement, in short an extension of metropolitan circulation. Frank Lloyd Wright once innocently predicted that «the new city will be nowhere, yet everywhere» (1977: 344); which can now be taken to mean that the urban habitat is a total interior and that beyond it there is no longer an «elsewhere» (Mazzoleni & Belfiore 1983: 26). In the postmodern context, of course, all the world is America---a single technotronic circuit, one speculative and ubiquitous city. In John Cournos's novel *The Wall,* Gombarov, the Jewish-American protagonist, expresses this sense of being imprisoned by the city of Philadelphia of the early twentieth century as follows: «And the whole stone city appeared to him as one vast cage, a maze of walls, and whichever way he walked there was no way out» (1921: 218). Gombarov's Philadelphia, of course, is also T.S. Eliot's «unreal city» of the wasteland which has exchanged all the representational values of the polis for a dynamics of constant change. If the traditional city, which refers back to the Renaissance ideal of the *urbs* as a single work of art (Argan 1983: 82-93), is based on quality and organic unity, the metropolis is based on quantity and geometrical extension. The passage from one to the other expresses a radical shift, a shift that characterizes the birth of a new epoch in which the metropolitan condition is normative and its morphology transcultural.

Perhaps the most distinctive feature of the modern city is its fluidity, its ability to devour space by legislating machine-induced velocity along its principal arteries. Topography for it is insignificant and this helps to explain why the real form of the metropolis is its very formlessness. In his autobiography *The Way It Was,* Harold Loeb recalls meeting with Marinetti, the Italian futurist poet, and the latter's enthusiasm for the new world: «The United States was his great admiration. Energy! Electricity! Acceleration! Vitality.» «I should have been thrilled but, perversely, I thought of Henry Adams,» Loeb says; adding, «I wondered when the speeding up process was going to stop» (1959: 41). Likewise, when Le Corbusier first gains sight of the «fantastic, almost mystical city» of New York, he cries out with equal European fervor, «Behold the temple of the new world» (1937; Ital. tr. 1975: 42). On this evidence he concludes, «The world is undergoing one of the great metamorphoses of its history» (42). Not surprisingly, the very physiognomy of New York, where «everything is moving, everything changing» (47), reflects in the eyes of Le Corbusier a «magic catastrophe» (50).

In reality, velocity only multiplies human absence and makes the materiality of things disappear. What is more, one cannot possess this type of city or claim it as «mine» since it has neither center nor coherence. It is this organization of space, so rationally regulated by the gridiron layout of American cities, that explains the «perversity» of Loeb's above allusion to Henry Adams, whose demystifying *Education* corrects Marinetti's exuberance: «The child born in 1900 would... be born into a new world which would not be a unity but a multiple» (1974: 42). The existential problem of orientation that Adams is hinting at is strictly related to urban anamorphosis and spatial fragmentation deriving from the city's grid-plan, as Waldo Frank also reveals when he protests, «A line can never express a life. Life is not linear... my existence cannot be limned in a Euclidean graph» (1973: 212). «In Europe, I had learned to absorb the spirit of a town by walking its streets,» he says (37). On the contrary, for the metropolitan type walking is a regressive experience. As a boy Frank used to know and love the sidewalks of New York, but as an adult he notes, «Today, the sidewalks are filets of human nerves lacerated by the perpetual city shrieks» (127). Between Frank's boyhood and manhood, a shift has occurred in the biology and the forms of *habitare*. A single urban element, the avenue, has become its sole *raison d'etre;* and with the accompanying automobile, dromocracy its reigning *logos*. In this habitat both Frank and Cournos's protagonist, Gombarov, «felt an Ishmael, a Pariah, a Wandering Jew» (Cournos 1922: 384).

This new conception of existence, according to which *«être c'est ne pas habiter»* (Virilio 1980: 28), informs the following urban experience described in Ludwig Lewisohn's autobiography *Up Stream* in which yet another Jewish-American protagonist journeys across New York:

> An *indifferent* acquaintance met me and *hustled* me to the nearest station of the Ninth Avenue «L.» We *climbed* the iron staircase, *scrambled* for tickets and were *jammed* into a car. It was the evening *rush hour* and we had barely *standing* room. The train *rattled* on its way to Harlem. At one Hundred and Sixteenth Street we *slid down* in the elevator to the street, *frantically dodged* people and vehicles across Eighth Avenue, turned south and west and stood presently before one of a row of three story houses *wedged* in between huge, dark buildings. They led me to a hall bedroom.... I put down my valise and took off my overcoat and *stood still,* quite *still....* I was in New York. I was *alone.* (1926: 120-21; emphases mine).

If in this passage (see my underlinings) kinetic energy drives everyone and everything forward, the train is the real agent, even if its mechanical movement is in turn predetermined by the rectilinear disposition of the streets. And just as the latter are marked by mere numbers, so too does movement along them suggest a quantitative process of addition. In terms of seeing and its correlative spatial object, Lewisohn's itinerary offers no topographical points of reference, no variety, since geometry has cancelled the face of topography. Even the spatial district of Harlem, it seems, has none of the distinguishing features that help to convert space into a series of places.

Not unlike Dos Passos's American youth, Lewisohn too remains rather passive during his urban journey and his participation is largely reduced to reaction. His passage from the *Geist* of the crowd to the solitude of his room is merely an issue of subtraction, for the crowd itself is only a numerical entity. Without extrapolating too much, one can intuit here that rapid transportation is meant to serve individuals as they exercise the mass man's functions of production and consumption, and not to increase the possibilities of socialization and communication. The tempo of the metropolis, of America, requires the self to be a *perpetuum mobile* in a highly organized culture of profit (Angenot 1979: 18-33), so that productive circulation is not only behind the physiognomy of the avenue and the space-conquering subway car, but also behind the crisis of *habitare*.

It is from within this «huge invisible man-trap» that Louis H. Sullivan (the creator of the first skyscraper) writes, «Later he sent forth his soul into the world and by and by his soul returned to him with an appalling message» (1956: 289). The human soul, like Sullivan's building frames, had become pure function. But if the technological city could not be humanized, then the human being must be technologized---by having him internalize the city. Perhaps nobody better than F. Scott Fitzgerald offers us such an acute insight into «that new thing--- the Metropolitan spirit» (1981: 21):

> Incalculable city.... To my *bewilderment,* I was adopted... as the archetype of what New York wanted.... There was already the tall white city of today, already the *feverish* activity of the boom, but there was a general inarticulateness.... I, or rather it was «we» now, did not know what New York expected of us and found it rather *confusing.* Within a few months after our *embarkation* on the Metropolitan venture we scarcely knew any more who we were and we hadn't a notion what we were.... a lot of rather *lost* and *lonely* people. The world of the picture actors was like our own.... *frayed nerves* were *strewn* everywhere; groups were held together by a generic *nervousness....* as the toiler must live in the city's belly, so I was compelled to live in its *disordered mind.* (23, 24, 28; my emphases).

Here the general intensification of the peculiar nervous life of the crowd---Georg Simmel would call it *Nervenleben* (Choay 1965; Ital. tr., 1973: 417-29)---is the theme and the vaporization of the self the result. The very sense of bewilderment is associated with the loss of a sense of place and erases the classical connotations of the voyage implied by the word «embarkation.» One could easily imagine a condition of floating on a phantasmagoric sea of phenomena if the objectual world itself had not disappeared from this scene. There is only «feverish activity» and confusion in what is presented as a rather abstract habitat. The world of concrete space, of objects, of the self as being-in-the-world, seems to have given way to a rarefied world of process which promises no peace. Materiality itself and the very idea of the body are forgotten. Indeed, in his autobiographical account «The Crack-up,» Fitzgerald describes the human ego as «an arrow shot from nothingness to nothingness» (1981: 40).

It is Le Corbusier, for that matter, who writes of his life in New York, «We are inside the whirlwind, we are the whirlwind, we ourselves a whirlwind, and we cannot even judge what is not a whirlwind» (80). William Carlos Williams was quite right when he said that «a man is indeed a city» (1967: 390). In short, the metropolis had drastically modified the structure of inhabited space in the United States, making it impossible to dwell in the modern world. As Francesco Dal Co says in his book *Abitare nel moderno,* «No *patria* is destined to the modern; thus, no shelter awaits the inhabitant of the metropolis and no house can ultimately be possessed by the nomad who lives in it» (1983: 11).

The problem of being a foreigner in one's own country, we can conclude, is evidently more than an ethnic issue, although the ethnic subject remains an ideal seismograph for registering the modern crisis. Ethnic discourse, on the other hand, is clearly imprisoned within the cultural morphology described above. In his novel *The Wall,* Cournos has his Jewish-American protagonist finally confess:

> His childhood in the Russian woods---how long ago
> it all seemed!---appeared to him now, in spite of its
> loneliness..., a thing of inexpressible beauty. It was
> all a fairy-tale, a dream, a myth. (30).

Gombarov's radical redefinition of the status of his past, his origins, his ancestors, and his former *patria* should not be considered in a negative or pathetic light, since the process of deterritorialization that he so vividly describes in the novel amounts in effect to a new type of ethnic sign circulation, the only type, actually, which is still critically valid in the contemporary context.

The City of Advertisement, the New Status of the Word

Before addressing Cournos's ethnic perspective as «fairy-tale» and «myth,» however, I would first like to discuss, even if briefly, the further transformation of American space into the «hyper-metropolis» (Mazzoleni & Belfiore: 37) or, if you will, the so-called postmodern condition. Since I have already referred to it, Dos Passos's *U.S.A.* trilogy will serve quite well for the rapid observations I wish to make here, especially with regard to the status of language; for the speech of the people seems to be its magical touchstone, if not the very tool, for any future transformation of American life. At any rate, Dos Passos obviously views the speech community as a transhistorical constructive reality, and language itself comes in for a great deal of metanarrative comment in the various sections and installments of the trilogy. Indeed, what strikes me as one of the major contexts in *U.S.A.* for evaluating the effectiveness of the word is Dos Passos's tracing of the birth of modern advertising and public relations.

The central as well as most memorable figure in the creation of this new institution is J. Ward Moorehouse, through whose efforts sloganism, jingoism, image-making, and the strategy of the cliché become the standard and dominant mode of communication in modern America as a burgeoning consumer society. It is Moorehouse who states that «the lack of properly distributed information is the cause of most of the misunderstandings in this world» (Vol. 1: 284); and on this basis the building of an information society controlled by the mass media becomes his fundamental objective. He is, though, by no means a mad scientist or a palimsest of Faust. On the contrary, he is merely an ordinary example of Pound's affirmation in Canto CXV that «the living were made of cardboard» (1975: 794). As one character notes, whenever J. W. talked, «it was as if he was rehearsing a speech» (Vol. II: 235); and as another puts it, but not so kindly, «The guy's nothing but a goddam megaphone...» (301).

In his own defense J. W. would have alluded to the need for «scientific publicity,» as he calls it (Vol. II: 315), and it is precisely because of his expertise in this new field that he is wanted in Paris during the war. There he sets out to keep up the morale of Americans in Europe by practicing his public relations rhetoric, by making the word perform as a mass media event. Thus, the war becomes «America's great opportunity» (Vol. 1: 285), although J. W. «talked about being patriotic and saving civilization» (342). As for the people, Mr. Rasmussen, J. W's chief assistant, says, «The public'll damn well do what it's told...» (Vol. II: 307).

There are, of course, a number of people who still believe in the traditional status of the word, who believe that reality is not entirely subordinated to the image, a mere *mise en scène* of the media; but these personages, almost exclusively consigned to the biographical sketches, are all defeated. John Reed, for example, still believes in the metaphysical correspondences of such abstract words as life, liberty, and the pursuit of happiness: «Reed was a Westerner and words meant what they said» (Vol. II: 37). Words stand for things. Fiction and history are two different realities for him. The biographical trajectory of President Woodrow Wilson is an even better example of the attempt to promote such ideal rhetoric as the New Freedom, Industrial Harmony, and Make the World Safe For Democracy, all slogans which Dick Savage and his friend would translate as «Blahblahblahblah» (Vol. II: 108-12), thus signaling the end of belief in the legitimacy of political discourse *tout court*. Significantly, before he became president, Wilson was «a teacher of rhetoric,» a man who «lived in a universe of words» (Vol. II: 249), but not in the same way as J. W. for whom the only reality is that created by the public relations image. No, for Wilson «God was the Word / and the Word was God» (249). But after the war and the peace of Versailles, he had his back to the wall, «talking to save his faith in words... talking to save his faith in himself, in his father's God» (255). As everbody knows, of course, Wilson ended up a ruined man, a bare shadow of his former self and, somewhat ironically, paralyzed to the point of hardly being able to speak.

Postwar America was already the creation of the J. Ward Moorehouses. In the Newsreel sections of the trilogy fact and fiction are equally reduced to the status of information; in the process reality is «derealized,» the image is already beyond the categories of the true and the false (Perniola: 1980). The world has indeed become Nietzsche's fable: for now everything is fiction. When in *Nineteen Nineteen* a character named Daughter is told, «New York's no place for illusions,» she replies, «It all looks kinder like a illusion to me» (Vol. II: 267). Just as the real is dissolved by its simulacrum, so too is the human subject. The news, the image, is all. When Reggie, one of J. W.'s employees, is rebuked for making a wisecrack about J. W.'s being ill, Reggie justly retorts, «After all J. Ward Moorehouse isn't a man... it's a name.... You can't feel sorry when a name gets sick» (Vol. III: 511). The trilogy's last attempt to express the old value of words and the traditional status of the human subject occurs in the penultimate «Camera Eye» section dealing with the execution of the two Italian immigrants Sacco and Vanzetti: «but do they know that the old words of the immigrants are being renewed in blood and agony tonight... the men in the deathhouse made the old words new before they died» (Vol. III: 469). But Wilson's defeat, like Randolph Bourne's, Paul Bunyan's, and Joe Hill's, is repeated once again, as the concluding words of this section admit: «we stand defeated America» (469). The explanation for this defeat should by now be evident, but Dick Savage, J.W.'s right-hand man, explains the pragmatics of the new type of semantic circulation once again towards the end of the trilogy and this time in the definitive terms of a nascent postmodern condition:

> Whether you like it or not, the molding of the public mind is one of the most important things that goes on in this country.... It's only through publicrelations work that business is protected from wildeyed cranks and demagogues who are always ready to throw a monkeywrench into the industrial machine. (Vol. III: 511).

As the Sacco and Vanzetti affair reveals, there is really no escape from the above cultural model; in the city of advertisement language, idealistically conceived, is in exile. The essence of culture is that which is created by the technics of the mass media. There is no longer anything behind the simulacrum: no prototype, no original; no authentic object or unique and unrepeatable subjectivity (Perniola: 121ff). By the second half of the twentieth century, all these factors were even further developed. In fact, the national map is now capable of realizing an updated version of the American dream, a hyperreal circulation of simultaneous communication in which the human subject, no longer hampered by a physical body, can be everywhere and yet nowhere at the same time. In his book *Esthétique de la disparation,* Paul Virilio calls this new potentiality the condition of *polutropos* or ubiquitous absence (28 - 29), for both subject and object are now disincarnated simulacra and can therefore be infinitely reproduced and multiplied. The very notion of linear time is also anachronistic within this postmodern episteme, since past and future are both technologically reduced to present time. The effects of this new technocracy can also be seen in the realm of cultural creation where spatial form has become a dominant narrative strategy. In the poetics of the novel, for example, synchronic relations have been given precedence over diachronic referentiality. Juxtaposition rather than causal sequence and fragmentation rather than perspectivism constitute the resulting logic of much contemporary fiction.

Postmodern Ethnic Semiosis

What the above postmodern condition means for the practice of ethnic discourse has already been hinted at by Cournos's protagonist, Gombarov; it now remains for me to make the new potentialities of the ethnic subject more explicit. Instead of using Henry Adams's negatively intended image of the multiverse to explain the contemporary organization of American culture, though, I find it more appropriate to speak of possible worlds, as linguists and semioticians do (Eco 1979: 122-31). Since it pertains strictly to the domain of interpretation, a possible world has no other foundation than that of the conceptual structures produced by discourse. As such, it is a set of hypotheses about what is possible, a series of propositional attitudes that function as a structural representation of concrete semantic realizations. In this context, authenticity is equivalent to the creation of meaning. There is indeed a plurality of different realities, but all of them have the status of a possible world.

The old distinction between that which is and that which is not, Borutti explains in her book *Significato,* is not an absolute one between real objects and imaginary non-objects, but a distinction between various ways of structuring the object (72). Both are possible objects of discourse for the mass media; both can be produced as simulacra. In a society where the «real» world has become predominantly an open series of possible worlds, ethnic discourse, insofar as it is intended as primordial and is dedicated to a strategy of recovering the so-called authentic culture of the ancestors, is actually a pseudo-discourse, a pathetic anthropology. In the postmodern context it is useless to speak of authentic as opposed to false ethnic culture, implying that only one deserves cultivation; it is useless to try to distinguish between existentially lived and symbolic ethnicity, as if the first were real and the latter were a mere sportive romp. Authenticity now pertains to the pragmatics of simulation rather than to a process of literal representation. For all practical purposes, traditional strategies limited to the tracing of past ethnic correspondences are dead; long live ethnic pragmatics. Ethnic fiction too is dead; long live ethnic semiosis.

There is, of course, an ethnic story to tell, but the ethnic subject must first learn to be at ease among signs. And given the history of American ethnogenesis, the world of signs---the world of absence---should be the ethnic subject's natural place. Here ethnic discourse is finally free to become a sober instrument of cultural construction without any regrets over a lost world of mimetic reproduction. The status of the ethnic sign is purely operative

132

in the postmodern framework, purely perfomative. To think otherwise would be to ignore the weak epistemology that constitutes its very strength. If one cannot dwell in the modern world, one can still dwell at the level of interpretation, as we shall see. In fact, ethnocultural construction is itself a possible world among others, a different strategy for creating a world of referents. In this light the ethnic sign functions as a working hypothesis for a possible action. And its range proves limitless exactly because the ethnic *verbum* has been disincarnated, stripped of its primordial and genealogical uniqueness: which is also why it is epistemologically weak. Only as such can everything imaginable under the sun be transformed into an ethnic sign, into a matter for ethnic semiosis. After all, the task of ethnic framing is not to name a world already known but to produce the same conditions of knowability as that which has already been named (Eco 1984: 208). Far from being confined to the ethnic encyclopedia as a set of fixed cultural contents to be continually reproposed with each new generation, the ethnic subject now plays freely with the encyclopedia in order to produce an ethno-critical interpretation of the present and of his possibilities in it.

The Ethnic Self as Catastrophic Subject

By «plays freely» I mean that in the postmodern context the ethnic sign is basically deterritorialized, to the extent that the old concept of identity as a «given of nature,» as a biographical unity, is no longer valid (Melucci 1983: 158).[1] In other words, as Gianni Vattimo says in *Al di là del soggetto,* the contemporary subject can no longer be considered a stable fact because the person as a center of identity and as organic form has been stripped of all such metaphysical trappings (198).

133

The self is an effect of the surface, a fiction, a construction, a linguistic stratagem, the result of a serious game of words and possible worlds. In short, he has no *Grund* outside of interpretation, which ultimately means that in order for the subject to be ethnic, he must perform ethnically, put into play his ethno-semiotic competence, defer existential facts to the model of ethnic semiosis which I discussed in chapter three.

In his work *Le Livre des Questions,* Jewish-French poet Edmond Jabès expresses this symbolic status of the self as follows: «To be able to respond: 'I belong to the race of words with which dwellings are built,' knowing well that this response is still a question, that this dwelling is always threatened (1963; Ital. tr., 1982: 34). But this sense of the subject's contingency and his precariousness as language reveals a corollary aspect in Cournos's novel *The Mask* where Semyon Gombarov's brother, Israel, thinks nothing of changing his name to Sam Carney when he learns «that it was an evil thing to be a Jew» (171-2). Dos Passos's J. W. Moorehouse, one will recall, made it clear that this business of naming in general is a mere question of strategic circulation. Face-work and not identity determines the new definitional model of the self, as expressed even by Eliot's Prufrock: «[T]o prepare a face to meet the faces that you meet» (see «The Love Song of J. Alfred Prufrock»). Cournos's John Gombarov, in fact, seems to catch on to this new fictional economy of things when he muses:

> How was one to put on a smile and yet seem to smile naturally? He practiced before a mirror; he tried to wear a continual smile, in order, as it were, to get his face used to it, to break it in to second nature, which, after all, is in so many people stronger than the first. (*The Wall:* 41).

For most immigrants in the United States, being American is like having a second nature; it is simply a matter of hiding one's original identity and accepting the dominant patterns of social behavior---thus the importance of the subtle *jeu* of stereotyping so prevalent in most American ethnic fiction. If the ethnic subject, A(non-A), is deterritorialized and postmodern identity is reduced to one-dimensional appearances and micro-segmental performances, ethnic semiosis has only to gain by it; for ethnic implication is uncontrollable to the extent that the ethnic subject is multiple and polymorphic (Sciolla 1983: 119-28). After John Gombarov has mastered American face-work, he is deeply pleased with his new ethnic possibility of seeing and yet not being seen:

> Gombarov was pleased...; he was even more pleased for not having been recognized as a Jew. It was so much easier to «get on» when one was not a Jew. Secretly he was pleased with being a Jew. Only he did not want to look like one. (*The Wall:* 180).

This obviously «weak» status of behavioral opacity and mobility which is so typical of the ethnic self in America actually has a boomerang effect in the postmodern context in that now the ethnic self is potentially a catastrophic subject. As a pluralized and multiform self, the ethnic's very instability as well as his access to an open series of possible worlds make him unpredictable and aleatory. No amount of sociological study can anticipate when this self will shift roles. Because he is both inside and outside of the dominant culture, his ethnic framing activity often becomes what surely must seem a contradictory strategy of producing ethnic discontinuity out of the very cultural continuum of the national map. Moreover, since identification and not identity regulates the postmodern combinatory *jeu,* the ethnic subject can also be said to perform according to the principle of role reversibility.[2] In other words, future ethnic activity cannot be predicted on the basis of past ethnic performances. I would like to quote at length an exemplary narrative exposition of the catastrophic potentiality of ethnic semiosis, as the positive nature of the ethnic subject's dislocation lies here---in an absence that remains. In Cournos's novel *The Mask* Gombarov's uncle Sroolik recounts an episode in his life as a Jewish peddler to prove his point that «the Jew in life had become an actor»:

> Afterward it occurred to him that if life were indeed a game, he would play it more subtly. Instead of getting into a so-called Jewish skin, especially prepared for Jews by Gentiles, he made up his mind one day... that it was by far the better plan to get into one of the skins prepared by Gentiles for themselves.
>
> It was March 17th---St. Patrick's day---and as he stood with his wares in one of New York's thoroughfares a gang of hoodlums, each with a green clover in the lapel of his coat, passed him by with a derisive guffaw. He felt his face grow pale.... Behind the hoodlums came a tall, well-built man, dressed like other men except for a large sombrero hat.... There was a green clover in the lapel of his coat. He... paused in front of the boy.... «Look here, my boy,» he said..., «I don't want to buy anything, but I like your face, and so I'm going to give a piece of good advice, gratis.... You see, I'm a circus cowboy and bronco-busting is more in my line. Now you wouldn't take me for one of God's own chosen people, would you? Well, I am. But one day I got tired of it.... Since then I've been everything under the sun.... Now I'm with a Wild West show, always on the road.... For all that I'm a Jew, though none of my pals know it.... And so, my boy, I say to you: Chuck it! Get your hair cut! Straighten your face out!.... If you must say *Shema Israel,* say it on the q.t. all to yourself....»
>
> And so you see I'm right in saying that being a Jew is a matter of occupation. (172-5).

Read as a postmodern demonstration of the new status of the ethnic subject, this episode reveals *in nuce* a qualitatively new framing economy. Most obviously, Cournos's Jewish cowboy has created a new ethnic space which, in reality, is a hermeneutical non-space in the culture of the national map. Simply put, he cannot be located ethnically, and there is no way of telling when his Jewishness will surface. As such, he is potentially a figure of eruption, a catastrophic subject. His ethnic appearances are spontaneous, aleatory, and shifting, while his «identity» is ambiguous, cryptic, and allotropic. There is no way of judging by external means whether his ethnic gaze connotes consensus or competition or conflict because the ethnic factor remains under his mask, not necessarily as an element of revolutionary explosion but as an equally radical act of implosion. By «implosion» I am referring to the structure of symbolic ambivalence inherent in the phenomenological guise of the mask where the ethnic gaze can mean everything and nothing.

As catastrophic subject, therefore, the ethnic self is uncodifiable; his ethnicity a mute and virtual language. Indeed, ethnic semiosis in the postmodern context generates a world of surplus signs and semantic excess which cannot but deregulate the principle of identity and non-contradiction upon which the characterological typology of the American allegory is founded (Galimberti 1983: 241-44). Dwelling positively and segmentally among a number of possible worlds, ethnic subjects like Cournos's Jewish cowboy will always represent a destabilizing factor for the dominant ideology of American identity and will always free meaning from its prison of a rigidly ordered code. Commenting on his identity crisis in his autobiography *An Ethnic at Large,* Jerre Mangione concludes:

> I resolved mine by becoming an ethnic at large, with one foot in my Sicilian heritage, the other in the American mainstream. By this cultural gymnastic stance I could derive strength from my past and a feeling of hope for my present. (369).

What Mangione is ever so innocently describing by

this con-fusing stance is nothing other than the ethnic subject as a devourer of transparent signs, a subject who at any given moment can reverse his position and float meanings from one possible world to another, thus creating semantic disorder and at times a cultural short-circuit. By inhabiting an ethno-symbolic universe and by practicing a framing semiotics that is willfully imprecise, that positively encourages the mixing up of various cultural codes, both Mangione and Cournos's ethnic cowboy, the real monsters in American society, mass together every variety of signifier that comes within their grasp while at the same time never definitively anchoring any of them to concrete things. This fictional play of metaphors, this symbolic game, is also exemplified in the Pan-Indian movement, where different tribes have decided to use the stereotypes imposed on them by white Americans in order to create a common political cause. The concept «Indian» is, of course, a stereotype; no such creature exists in reality. There really is no common Indian identity, culture, or language (Feest 1983: 93-5). In the postmodern context, however, the Narragansetts of the northeast are not in the least ashamed of their use of the Sioux war dance to attract tourists and fill their coffers with dollars. The issue at stake here is not cultural recovery or a literal return to one's ancestors but ethnic production and reversibility. Mimetic representation is indeed an important critical strategy, especially when the diaphragm of quotation marks is used.

Ethnic mimesis, as we have seen above, is also a consciously parasitical attitude of subaltern survival without any false foundational pretenses. As Michel Serres points out in his compelling book *Le parasite,* «I do not know if mimicry is completely parasitical, but it is a necessary ruse for the thief, the foreigner, and the invited guest...» (1980: 272). Through mimetic politics, the ethnic subject identifies with his host and is thus accepted in American culture as American, while the ethnic factor often remains prepolitical, apolitical, or simply a private matter. In this way the ethnic self pretends to dwell in America, even though he conceals an external perspective within the social system. This elusiveness of the ethnic subject is explained by Serres in the following way:

> The action of the parasite is to seek relationship....
> He is included in the master's own home, he is dis-
> tributively included in all relations. He intercepts
> all the connections among all places. He catches all
> that flows.... He is *a* but not only *a*. He is also *b*....
> *A* is *b,* which must be demonstrated. (1983: 278).

It seems to me that we have now come full circle or, to keep up the motif of my title, we have now gone through the glass darkly, to the other, unofficial topology of American culture: the city on the hill without lights, the nocturnal banquet, the non-A of American identity that makes all if not the only difference in the national map, the space of the symbol where clear and distinct cultural correspondences are obfuscated by ethnic confusion, the realm of the local which cannot be reduced to the general flow.

Postmodern Ethnic Sapientia

In the culture of the simulacrum, the ethnic self cannot literally recover his lost origins or solve the global problem of *habitare* by returning to a preteletronic past. Deterritorialized, the ethnic subject dwells in a series of possible worlds; ethnic semiosis concerns «*non spazio, sed sapientia*» (Pound, Canto CV). Although the ethnic subject cannot escape the effects of the national map, he is surely in a privileged position to interpret it by subjecting American facts to a different self-reflective *jeu*. Here the local and marginal condition becomes the ethnic's very strength. Is not this one of the main reasons why ethnicity has become such a popular as well as populist filter for questioning the very way in which contemporary social experience is organized? As Edmond Jabès says in *Dal deserto al libro,* «To question is to refuse limits» (Mecatti 1984: 42). Ethnic semiosis establishes its own hierarchy of significance through a constructive strategy of ethnic interrogation. Indeed, in a culture without a historical memory, where the crisis of identity and the crisis of memory are coterminous, remembering is itself a central category of the ethnic project. By interrogating the *traditio* of his ancestors, the ethnic subject opens a new inferencing field in which he can re-present the crisis of cultural foundations in a critical light.

Far from expressing nostalgia for the center, for the global map, he revels in the realm of the local in its symbolic guise, in the realm of lost origins where facts are historicized through the ethno-semiotic gaze. In the final count, therefore, the efficaciousness of ethnic subjectivity has nothing to do with repossessing the global map. Its strength lies in its local weakness, as Jabès confirms in *Le Livre des Questions:*

> Turning to me, the brothers of my race said:
> «You are not a Jew. You don't attend the synagogue.»
> Addressing the brothers of my race, I replied:
> «I carry the synagogue in my breast.» (Ital. tr.: 64-5).

In much the same tone, Isaac Bashevis Singer recounts in his autobiography *Lost in America* that he passed from being a historical person to the status of one of his fictional characters:

> I fantasized that I was already dead, one of those legendary corpses which, instead of resting in the cemetery, leave their graves to reside in the world of chaos. I had described such living dead in my stories and now in my imagination I had become one of my own protagonists. (1981: 15).

Torn from his cultural humus, Singer's real self died. When he finally gets to America, he clings to the past, for «I could feel that some mental catastrophe was taking place here, some mutation for which there was no name in my vocabulary, not even a beginning of a notion» (107). In America Singer is lost, disoriented, lives in a non-place, remains an invisible man, but it is the ethnic factor which allows him to pretend to dwell in the modern condition:

> Someone had once advised me to always carry a compass.... A compass wouldn't have helped me. It would only have confused me further.... I suffer from a kind of disorientation complex.... The fact is that it was inherited.... In our house there hovered the fear of the outside, of gentile language, of trains, cars, of the hustle and bustle of business, even of Jews who had dealings with lawyers, the police, could speak Russian or even Polish. I had gone away from God, but not from my heritage. (117-18).

Out of this genealogical clay, Singer is able to invent a possible world. But in order to understand what this condition of nomadism actually means, we must penetrate this parable from Jabès's *Le Livre des Questions:*

> The well which I draw from is on Jewish land.
> My story takes its origins from the well.
> The well which I draw from is on Jewish land.
> On its well-curb my brothers sit.
> . . . .
> My brothers have lost their well.
> I will give you back your well. (Ital. tr.: 63).

Because of this very relation *in absentia,* ethnic semiosis creates a necessary fiction. Fable becomes possible where history has failed. Once in America, Singer's real dwelling becomes a verbal construct, and it is not a matter of ethnic continuism but of continuity as a radical questioning of contemporary American experience. Outside of his interpretative acts, the ethnic subject may even slip back into anonymity and be swallowed up by the larger culture.

141

But the ethnic remains semiotically strong because of his relationship with his originating cultural *traditio* which, as an absent presence, solicits ethnic interpretation in a metacultural space that is nowhere and everywhere at the same time. In his poem «Nostalgia» Italo-American-Canadian poet Pier Giorgio Di Cicco writes:

> under a few cold lilies, my father dreams
> cicadas in vallemaio. I am sure of it,
> he left me that, and a poem that is only a
> dream of cicadas.... (1979: 48).

Here memory as project is quite explicit, and where this floating strategy leads to Di Cicco suggests at the end of the poem: «I am a little marvellous, with the sunken / heart of exiles.» From this symbolic vantage point the ethnic sign cannot but be dispersive, supplementary, and polymorphic, but the competence for producing ethnic discourse is spelled out brilliantly in Di Cicco's poem «Remembering Baltimore, Arezzo»:

> I am not alone, I have never been alone. Ghosts are
> barking in my eyes, their soft tears washing us down
> to baltimore, out the chesapeake, round the atlantic,
> round the world, back where we started from, a
> small town in the shade of cypress, with nowhere to
> go but be still again. (10).

One can see working in this passage the genealogical impulse, a politics of memory, the double perspectivism of the subject, and the originating ancestral ghosts. But the poem goes even further in clarifying the particular *jeu* of ethnic reflexivity and its potentially critical status:

> It is a way of saying twentyfive years and some german
> bombs have made for roses in a backyard that we cry
> over, like some film which is too maudlin to pity and
> yet is the best we have to feel human about. (10).

There is no totalizing stratagem in these lines, only a kind of ethnic challenge in a minor genealogical key.

What one does find, though, is an originating source of cultural difference which is the tomb of the immigrant father. The tomb not only precedes but makes possible the poet-son's act of ethnic reflection. Ethnic semiosis, then, is a way of thinking differently by thinking the difference, and in the postmodern American framework this may be all the difference there is: a particular form of discourse, of evaluating the agency of the subject, of holding one's ground against the map of national circulation. It is fitting to conclude now with these words from the Italo-Canadian poet Antonino Mazza:

> If the dream doesn't stop, if the word,
> if the house
> is in the word and we, by chance, should meet,
> my house is your house, take it. (1984).

NOTES

Chapter One

[1] For an excellent study of James's experimental drama of seeing, see Sergio Perosa's book *Henry James and the Experimental Novel* (1978).

Chapter Two

[1] For this spatial approach to the question of identity I have relied heavily on the work of Michel Serres. See here his essay «Discours et parcours,» (1977).

[2] In his book *Regeneration Through Violence,* Richard Slotkin further confirms what I am attempting to establish in this chapter: «The English colonists had to remake their values, their concepts of law and religion, and their images of their role and place in the universe in order to survive in the wilderness. This necessity was difficult to acknowledge, since the colonists felt it their duty to remain loyal to their English heritage. It was far easier to define their cultural identity by negative means, through attacking or condemning alien elements in their society, by casting out heretics like Roger Williams and John Underhill... The Indian wars, in which culture was pitted against culture, afforded a perfect opportunity for this sort of definition by repudiation. In opposing the Indian culture, the Puritan symbolically affirmed his Englishness.» (Slotkin 1973: 22).

[3] As P.D.A. Harvey notes in his book *The History of Topographical Maps:* «When we speak of symbol-maps, diagram-maps, picture-maps, we are not really speaking of maps at all---they are simply the nearest approach that particular societies achieved to the concept of cartography that was attained only with the production of the scale-map....It is significant that there was no word for a map in any European language until the Renaissance; there was no word for a map because maps did not exist.» (Harvey 1980: 173).

[4] How important maps were in proving rival political claims to colonial territories can be seen by investigating the early colonial maps by such pivotal cartographers as Herman Moll and John Mitchell. (See Schwartz and Ehrenberg 1980: 135, 142, 159-60).

Chapter Three

[1] For a working definition of «possible world,» I have relied on Umberto Eco, *Lector in fabula* (1979). Since this concept plays an important role in my fourth chapter, and not really before, I refer the reader to it for an extensive treatment.

Chapter Four

[1] For a further discussion of this new conception of the self, see Alberto Izzo (1983), who relies heavily on the book *The Homeless Mind: Modernization and Consciousness* by Peter Berger, Brigitte Berger, Hansfried Kellner (New York: Random House, 1973) where it is written: «Biography is perceived both as a migration through diverse social worlds and as the consequent realization of a large number of possible identities.» (Quoted in Izzo 1983: 146).

[2] For a discussion of the principle of reversibility, see Ricolfi (1983: 214-7); see also L. Gallino (1983) for a discussion of the differences between identity and identification.

145

BIBLIOGRAPHY

Adams, Henry (1974). *The Education of Henry Adams,* Ernest Samuels (ed.). Boston: Houghton Mifflin Co.

Alter, Robert (1981). *The Art of Biblical Narrative.* New York: Basic Books, Inc.

Angelou, Maya (1978). *I Know Why the Caged Bird Sings.* New York: Bantam Books.

Angenot, Marc (1979). «Jules Verne: the last happy utopianist.» *Science Fiction, A Critical Guide,* Patrick Parrinder (ed.), 18-33. London: Longman Paperback.

Argan, Giulio Carlo (1983). *Storia dell'arte come storia della città.* Rome: Editori Riuniti.

Argan, Giulio Carlo (1984). «Così Roma è diventata Roma.» In «Tuttolibri,» *La Stampa,* Feb. 11, p. 4.

Bachelard, Gaston (1957). *La poétique de l'espace.* Paris: Presses Universitaires de France. (Ital. tr., *La poetica dello spazio,* Bari: Dedalo libri, 1975).

Bateson, Gregory (1972). *Steps to an Ecology of Mind.* Chandler Publishing Company. (Ital. tr., *Verso un'ecologia della mente,* Milan: Adelphi, 1976).

Beaugrande, Robert de & Wolfgang Dressler (1981). *Introduction to Text Linguistics.* London: Longman Paperback.

Bender, Thomas (1982). *Toward an Urban Vision.* Baltimore: Johns Hopkins Paperbacks.

Birnbaum, Gudrun (1983). «The New Ethnicity of the 1970's in the U.S.» *Le facteur ethnique aux Etats-Unis et au Canada,* Monique Lecomte & Claudine Thomas (eds.), 37-46. Lille: Presses de l'Université de Lille III.

Boelhower, William (1981). «The Immigrant Novel as Genre.» *MELUS,* Vol. 8, No. 1, Spring, 3-14.

Boelhower, William (1982). *Immigrant Autobiography in the*

United States. Verona: Essedue Edizioni.

Borutti, Silvana (1983). *Significato.* Bologna: Zanichelli.

Brown, Dee (1972). *Bury My Heart at Wounded Knee.* London: Pan Books Ltd.

Cacciari, Massimo (1973). *Metropolis.* Rome: Officina Edizioni.

Cagidemetrio, Alide (1983). *Verso il West.* Vicenza: Neri Pozza Editore.

Catani, A. Maria, ed. (1983). *Antologia selvaggia, i primi incontri con i bianchi.* Florence: Sansoni.

Cournos, John (1919). *The Mask.* London: Methuen.

Cournos, John (1921). *The Wall.* London: Methuen.

Cournos, John (1922). *Babel.* New York: Boni and Liveright.

Crèvecoeur, J. Hector St. John de (1957). *Letters from an American Farmer.* New York: Dutton Paperback.

Dal Co, Francesco (1983). *Abitare nel moderno:* Bari: Laterza.

Deleuze, Gilles & Félix Guattari (1980). *Mille plateaux.* Paris: Les Editions de Minuit.

Deloria, Vine (1975). «Indian Humor.» *Literature of the American Indian: Views and Interpretations,* Abraham Chapman (ed.), 152-69. New York: New American Library.

Derleth, August (1943). *Wind Over Wisconsin.* New York: Charles Scribner's Sons.

Di Cicco, Pier Giorgio (1979). *The Tough Romance.* Toronto: McClelland and Stewart.

Di Donato, Pietro (1939). *Christ in Concrete.* New York: Bobbs-Merrill Company.

Dos Passos, John (1969). *U.S.A.* trilogy, 3 Vols. New York: Signet Paperback.

Eco, Umberto (1979). *Lector in fabula.* Milan: Bompiani.

Eco, Umberto (1984). *Semiotica e filosofia del linguaggio.* Turin: Einaudi.

Feest, Christian (1983): «Indianness and Ethnicity.» *Le facteur ethnique aux Etats-Unis et au Canada,* Monique Lecomte & Claudine Thomas (eds.), 89-98. Lille: Presses de l'Université de Lille III.

Fitzgerald, F. Scott (1981). *The Crack-up, with other pieces and stories.* New York: Penguin Books.

Frank, Waldo (1973). *Memoirs of Waldo Frank,* Alan Trachtenberg (ed.). Massachusetts: University of Massachusetts Press.

Fuchs, Daniel (1961). *Three Novels.* New York: Basic Books, Inc.

Galimberti, Umberto (1983). *Il corpo.* Milan: Feltrinelli.

Galimberti, Umberto (1984). *La terra senza male.* Milan: Feltrinelli.

Gallino, Luciano (1983): «Identità, identificazione, relazioni seriali e alternanze.» *Complessità sociale e identità,* L. Balbo, F. Barbano, L. Gallino, *et. al.* (eds.), 227-38. Milan: Franco Angeli Editore.

Gleason, Philip (1981). «American Identity and Americanization.» *Harvard Encyclopedia of American Ethnic Groups,* Stephan Thernstrom (ed.), 31-58. Cambridge: The Belknap Press of Harvard.

Gliozzi, Giuliano (1977). *Adamo e il nuovo mondo.* Florence: La Nuova Italia Editrice.

Goffman, Erving (1967). *Interaction Ritual.* Garden City: Doubleday & Co., Inc.

Goffman, Erving (1974). *Frame Analysis.* New York: Harper, Colophon Book.

Green, John C. (1971). *La morte di Adamo,* L. Sosio, Ital. tr. Milan: Feltrinelli.

Greimas, Algirdas (1983). *Du Sens II.* Paris: Editions du Seuil.

Hamilton, Charles, ed. (1950). *Cry of the Thunderbird.* New York: Macmillan Publishing Co., Inc. (Ital. tr., *Sul sentiero di guerra,* Milan: Feltrinelli, 1982).

Hansen, Diana & Lucio Ranucci, eds. (1977). *Indiani d'America.* Rome: Savelli.

Harvard Encyclopedia of American Ethnic Groups (1981), Stephan Thernstrom (ed.). Cambridge: The Belknap Press of Harvard.

Harvey, P.D.A. (1980). *The History of Topographical Maps.* London: Thames and Hudson Ltd.

Heidegger, Martin (1965). «Building Dwelling Thinking.» *L'ur-*

banisme. Utopies et réalités, Françoise Choay (ed.). Paris: Edition du Seuil, (Ital. tr., *La città. Utopie e realtà,* 437-43, Turin: Einaudi, 1973).

Helprin, Mark (1982). *Ellis Island and Other Stories.* New York: Delta.

Himes, Dell (1981). *«In vain I tried to tell you.»* Philadelphia: University of Pennsylvania Press.

Honour, Hugh (1975). *The New Golden Land.* New York: Pantheon Books.

Izzo, Alberto (1983). «Il concetto di 'mondo vitale.'» *Complessità sociale e identità,* L. Balbo, F. Barbano, L. Gallino, *et al.* (eds.), 132-49. Milan: Franco Angeli Editore.

Jabès, Edmond (1963). *Le Livre des Questions.* Sixth Book. Paris: Gallimard. (Ital. tr., *Il libro delle interrogazioni,* Reggio Emilia: Elitropia, 1983).

Jacob, Christian (1980). «Écritures du monde.» *Cartes et figures de la terre,* 104-19. Paris: Centre Georges Pompidou.

James, Henry (1968). *The American Scene.* Bloomington: Indiana University Press.

James, Henry (1968b). «The Art of Fiction.» *Selected Literary Criticism,* Morris Shapira (ed.), 78-97. Harmondsworth: Peregrine Books.

Jones, Howard Mumford (1965). *O Strange New World.* New York: The Viking Press.

Kingston Maxine Hong (1977). *The Woman Warrior.* Harmondsworth: Penguin Books.

Le Corbusier (1937). *Quand les cathédrales étaient blanches.* Paris: Editions Plon. (Ital. tr., *Quando le cattedrali erano bianche,* Faenza: Faenza Editrice, 1975).

Lewisohn, Ludwig (1926). *Up Stream.* New York: The Modern Library Publishers.

Lincoln, Kenneth (1983). «Native American Literatures.» *Smoothing the Ground, Essays on Native Amreican Oral Literature,* Brian Swann (ed.), 3-38. Berkeley: University of California Press.

Loeb, Harold (1959). *The Way It Was.* New York: Criterion Books.

Mangione, Jerre (1942). *Mount Allegro*. Cambridge, Mass.: The Riverside Press.

Mangione, Jerre (1978). *An Ethnic at Large*. New York: G.P. Putnam's Sons.

Marramao, Giacomo (1984). *Potere e secolarizzazione*. Rome: Editori Riuniti.

Mazza, Antonino (1984). «Our House is in a Cosmic Ear.» Poem published in pamphlet form by the poet.

Mazzoleni, Donatella & Pasquale Belfiori (1983). *Metapolis*. Rome: Officina Edizioni.

Mecatti, Stefano, ed. (1984). *Edmond Jabès. La voce della scrittura*. Florence: Sansoni.

Melucci, Alberto (1983). «Identità e azione collettiva.» *Complessità sociale e identità*, L. Balbo, F. Barbano, L. Gallino, et. al. (eds.), 150-66. Milan: Franco Angeli Editore.

Melville, Herman (1981). *Moby-Dick*. Berkeley: University of California Press. (Based on the Arion Press Edition, '79).

Miceli, Silvana (1982). *In nome del segno*. Palermo: Sellerio editore.

Miller, James, ed. (1956). *The American Puritans*. New York: Anchor Books.

Moberg, Vilhelm (1961). *The Settlers,* Gustaf Lannestock, tr. New York: Popular Library.

Momaday, N. Scott (1976). *The Names*. New York: Harper & Row, Publishers.

Morrison, Toni (1978). *Song of Solomon*. New York: Signet, New American Library.

Mumford, Lewis (1952). *Art and Technics*. New York: Columbia University Press.

Norburg-Schulz, Christian (1971). *Existence, Space and Architecture*. Oslo. (Ital. tr., *Esistenza, spazio e architectura,* Rome: Officina Edizioni, 1982).

Olson, Charles (1947). *Call Me Ishmael*. (Ital. tr., *Chiamatemi Ismaele,* Parma: Guanda, 1972).

Ostendorf, Berndt (1983). «Ghetto Literature, or: What Makes Ethnic Literature Ethnic?» *Le facteur ethnique aux Etats-Unis et au Canada,* Monique Lecomte & Claudine Thomas (eds.), 149-62: Lille: Presses de l'Université de Lille III.

Pagano, Jo (1943). *Golden Wedding*. New York: Random House.

Pellegrini, Angelo (1956). *Americans by Choice*. New York: The Macmillan Company.

Perniola, Mario (1980). *La società dei simulacra*. Bologna: Cappelli Editore.

Perosa, Sergio (1978). *Henry James and the Experimental Novel*. Charlottesville: University of Virginia Press. (Republished in 1984 by New York University Press).

Pignatelli, Paola Coppola (1982). *Spazio e immaginario*. Rome: Officina Edizioni.

Potter, David (1975). *History and American Society*, Don E. Fehrenbacher (ed.). New York: Oxford University Press.

Pound, Ezra (1975). *The Cantos*. London: Faber and Faber.

Poyatos, Fernando (1983). *New Perspectives in Nonverbal Communication*. Toronto: Pergamon Press.

Prontera, Francesco (1983). *Geografia e geografi nel mondo antico*. Bari: Laterza.

Quiett, Glenn Chesney (1965). *They Built the West*. New York: Cooper Square Publishers, Inc.

Reps, John W. (1969). *Town Planning in Frontier America*. Princeton: Princeton University Press. (Ital. tr., *La costruzione dell'America urbana*, Milan: Franco Angeli Editore, 1976).

Ricolfi, Luca (1983). «Self deception. Elster e Luhmann: due critiche del paradigma utilitarista.» *Complessità sociale e identità*, L. Balbo, F. Barbano, L. Gallino, *et. al.* (eds.), 199-226. Milan: Franco Angeli Editore.

Rölvaag, Ole (1927). *Giants in the Earth*, Lincoln Colcord and author, trs. New York: Harper & Brothers, Perennial Library.

Rölvaag, Ole (1931). *Their Fathers' God*, Trygve Ager, tr. New York: Harper & Bros.

Rossi-Landi, Ferruccio (1968). *Il linguaggio come lavoro e come mercato*. Milan: Bompiani.

Rothschild, Joseph (1981). *Ethnopolitics*. New York: Columbia

University Press. (Ital. tr., *Etnopolitica*, Milan: SugarCo Edizioni, 1984).

Schwartz, Seymour I. & Ralph E. Ehrenberg (1980). *The Mapping of America*. New York: Harry N. Abrams, Inc., Publishers.

Sciola, Loredana (1983). «Il concetto di identità in sociologia.» *Complessità sociale e identità*, L. Balbo, F. Barbano, L. Gallino, *et. al.* (eds.), 101-131. Milan: Franco Angeli Editore.

Serres, Michel (1977). «Discours et parcours.» *L'identité*, Claude Lévi-Strauss (ed.). Paris: Editions Grasset et Rasquelle.

Serres, Michel (1980). *Le parasite*. Paris: Grasset.

Serres, Michel (1980b). *Le passage du nord-ouest. Hermes V.* Paris: Les Editions de Minuit.

Shirley, Rodney W. (1983). *The Mapping of the World*. London: The Holland Press Limited.

Simmel, Georg (1965). «The Big Cities and the Life of the Spirit.» *L'urbanisme. Utopies et réalités*, Françoise Choay (ed.). Paris: Editions du Seuil. (Ital. tr., *La città. Utopie e realtà,* 417-29, Turin: Einaudi, 1973).

Singer, Isaac Bashevis (1981). *Lost in America*. Garden City: Doubleday & Co., Inc.

Sini, Carlo (1982). *Kinesis. Saggio di interpretazione*. Milan: Spirali Edizioni.

Slotkin, Richard (1973). *Regeneration Through Violence: The Mythology of the American Frontier, 1600-1860*. Middleton: Wesleyan University Press.

Smith, Alice E. (1973). *The History of Wisconsin*, Vol. I. Madison: State Historical Society of Wisconsin.

Smith, Anthony D. (1981). *The Ethnic Revival*. Cambridge: Cambridge University Press. (Ital. tr., *Il revival etnico*, Bologna: Il Mulino, 1984).

Smith, John (1970). *Captain John Smith's History of Virginia,* David Freeman Hawke (ed.). New York: The Bobbs-Merrill Company, Inc.

Sollors, Werner (1981). «Literature and Ethnicity.» *Harvard Encyclopedia of American Ethnic Groups*, Stephan Thernstrom (ed.), 647-65. Cambridge: The Belknap Press of Harvard.

Sollors, Werner (1981b). «Theory of American Ethnicity, or: '? S ethnic?/Ti and AMERICAN/TI, DE OR UNITED (W) STATES S SI AND THEOR?'» *American Quarterly,* Vol. 33, No. 3, 257-83.

Sowell, Thomas (1981). *Ethnic America.* New York: Basic Books, Inc., Publishers.

Steiner, Edward (1914). *From Alien to Citizen.* New York Fleming H. Revell Co.

Stilgoe, John R. (1982). *Common Landscape of America, 1580 to 1845.* New Haven: Yale University Press.

Sullivan, Louis H. (1956). *The Autobiography of an Idea.* New York: Dover Publications.

Swann, Brian, ed., (1983). «Introduction» to *Smoothing the Ground,* xi-xix. Berkeley: University of California Press.

Tomasi, Mari (1949). *Like Lesser Gods.* Milwaukee: The Bruce Publishing Company.

Turri, Eugenio (1979). *Semiologia del paesaggio italiano.* Milan: Longanesi & Co.

Vagaggini, Vincenzo (1982). *Le nuove Geografie.* Genoa: Herodote Edizioni.

Vattimo, Gianni (1981). *Al di là del soggetto.* Milan: Feltrinelli.

Vergara, Joe (1968). *Love and Pasta.* New York: Harper & Row, Publishers.

Virilio, Paul (1977). *Vitesse et Politique.* Paris: Editions Galilée. (Ital. tr., *Velocità e politica,* Milan: Multhipla Edizioni, 1981).

Virilio, Paul (1980). *Esthétique de la disparition.* Saint-Amand, Cher: Editions Balland.

Wahl, François (1980). «le désir d'espace.» *Cartes et figures de la terre.* Paris: Centre George Pompidou.

Williams, Edwin, ed. (1849). *Stetesman's Manual,* 4 Vols. New York: Edward Walker.

Williams, William Carlos (1967). *The Autobiography of William Carlos Williams.* New York: New Directions.

Williams, William Carlos (1971). *In the American Grain.* Harmondsworth: Peregrine Bks.

Winther, Sophus Keith (1936). *Take All to Nebraska*. New York: Macmillan Co.

Wittgenstein, Ludwig (1922). *Tractatus Logico-Philosophicus,* Ital. tr., Turin: Einaudi, 1964.

Wright, Frank Lloyd (1977). *An Autobiography*. New York: Horizon Press.

Wroth, Lawrence C. (1970). *The Voyages of Giovanni da Verrazzano*. New Haven: Yale University Press.